Great Second Acts

GREAT SECOND ACTS

In Praise of Older Women

Marlene Wagman-Geller

Mango Publishing

CORAL GABLES

For permission requests, please contact the publisher at:

Mango Publishing Group
2850 Douglas Road, 3rd Floor
Coral Gables, FL 33134 USA
info@mango.bz

For special orders, quantity sales, course adoptions and
corporate sales, please email the publisher at sales@mango.
bz. For trade and wholesale sales, please contact Ingram
Publisher Services at customer.service@ingramcontent.com
or +1.800.509.4887.

Great Second Acts: In Praise of Older Women

Library of Congress Cataloging
ISBN: (print) 978-1-63353-822-1 (ebook) 978-1-63353-823-8

Library of Congress Control Number: 2018956901

BISAC category code: BIO022000
BIOGRAPHY & AUTOBIOGRAPHY / Women

Printed in the United States of America

In praise of older women who say to old age what Madeleine told the tiger at the zoo: "Pooh, pooh."

And to the praise of my women—my mother, Gilda Wagman, and my daughter, Jordanna Shyloh Geller.

"Age cannot wither her, nor custom stale her infinite variety..."

William Shakespeare (1606)
Antony and Cleopatra

TABLE OF CONTENTS

PROLOGUE

The Best Is Yet to Be

With the optimism of youth, there is an inherent belief that, in the words of Dorothy from *The Wizard of Oz*, "The dreams that you dare to dream really do come true." However, as the calendar pages turn, our aspirations tend to recede into the distance, placed on the back burner by financial survival, child-rearing, and male maintenance. Then, in a dizzying blur, we gasp at the pigment-free image staring back from the mirror, reminding us how quickly time passes. It is essential that we do not go gentle into our twilight years. Ladies who experience late-in-life reinvention are the embodiment of what Antony said about Cleopatra: "Age cannot wither her / Nor custom stale / Her infinite variety."

Growing up in Toronto, Canada, my holy grail was to have my name on the spine of a book, having a seat in my own version of the Algonquin Round Table. Life did not play out that way. (Surprise, surprise.) While waiting to publish the great Canadian novel, heir apparent of Margaret Atwood, I became a high school English teacher. Although pouring knowledge into young minds is a noble pursuit, my dream of authorship haunted me.

In 1986, I moved to San Diego, had my dear daughter, and taught high school English. Over the decades, I penned various novels and received enough rejection slips to wallpaper Buckingham Palace. My aborted attempts gave me a ringside seat to the Boulevard of Broken Dreams. The proverb "Hope may be a good breakfast but is a bad dinner" held true. And then serendipity walked in: my second act. In 2008, after making substantial inroads on my biblically allotted threescore years and ten, Penguin published my first book, *Once Again to Zelda: The Stories Behind Literature's Most*

The realization of my dream proved the truth of the old saying, "Better late than never."

Conventional wisdom holds that, if a person does not write *Wuthering Heights,* paint *Starry Night,* or climb Mt. Everest before a varicose vein makes its appearance, chances are it ain't gonna happen. The over-fifty set need not compare themselves to those who set the world aflame before their twenties: the French Joan of Arc was freeing her country from the British at age eighteen; the Romanian Nadia Comaneci received three gold Olympic medals at age fourteen; the Pakistani Malala Yousafzai won the Nobel Prize at age seventeen. Our youth-obsessed culture, which tends to assume ingenuity wanes as the years go by, fosters this idea. Hence, late bloomers arm-wrestle with powerful prejudice as they face those who think they are no longer viable. The message: Age delivers, along with Poligrip and orthopedic shoes, a drying of the creative juices. In such a climate, older folk may easily succumb to the belief that the great imaginative leap remains in the realm of yesteryear. The mindset becomes that it is too late, followed by the painful pang of it-could-have-been. Dorothy Parker expressed this sentiment when she wrote, "Time doth flit; oh shit."

The nineteenth-century novel was the contemporary soap opera, and Charles Dickens did a number on older gals with his depiction of Miss Havisham in his novel *Great Expectations.* Jilted at the altar, her mansion became a mausoleum; in a decaying wedding dress with matching white hair, she existed in perpetual mourning. Her cinematic heir, Norma Desmond, dwelt on the aptly named Sunset Boulevard. Rather than look ahead, she anxiously awaited the return of a parade that had long passed her by. Another fictional character that helped foster the stereotype of women in their later years as unable to retain their marbles was Bette Davis's role in the movie *Whatever Happened to Baby Jane?* The answer to the title's rhetorical question: She became a madwoman not confined to the attic and became the worst a lady can be in her twilight years—delusional, homicidal, sadistic. The image of the meal she served her sister, which consisted of a pet bird, is not one that can ever be unseen. In contrast, the non-celluloid Bette retained her clarity and sagely remarked, "Old age is not for sissies."

Fortunately, the long-established paradigm of older women being beyond our expiration date for achievement and sanity has received a well-deserved shakedown as women have obtained late-in-life success. After all, the rings on a trunk make for the most majestic of trees. An important idea to keep in mind—and yes, we still have one—is that the golden years can be rewarding creatively, emotionally, and romantically.

Maggie Kuhn, an octogenarian who proved frail bodies can mask iron spirits, called herself a little old woman. She celebrated her forced retirement—a gesture of out with the old and in with the new—by founding the Gray Panthers, a name derived from the radical Black Panthers. In 1972, she told the *New York Times,* "I have gray hair, many wrinkles, and arthritis in both hands. And I celebrate my freedom from bureaucratic restraints that once held me." Kuhn refused to be defined by the year on her birth certificate.

Another kidney-punch to time was Sue Ellen Cooper's Red Hat Society that proved girls just wanna have fun. Her organization is a nod to matrons who have earned their stripes, a.k.a. wrinkles and bags. The red hats are a variation of a Purple Heart: proof positive they have survived all life has dished out.

In China, the elderly members of the family are venerated patriarchs, while in Western cultures, senior citizen homes proliferate. Perhaps the finger of blame should be pointed at the German siblings Wilhelm and Johann Grimm. In their classic fairy tales, the villain was the ancient crone. She was the one whose version of hospitality was to shove Hansel and Gretel into the oven, to imprison Rapunzel in a tower, to turn

into a hag to trick Snow White into eating the poisoned apple.
The reason why Snow White's stepmother replaced maternal
nurturing with malice is that she was no longer the fairest in
the land. Grimm indeed.

Fortunately, the world has made strides and is more
accepting of its seniors. Anna Mary Robertson, forever known
as Grandma Moses, was in her late seventies when arthritis
made her beloved embroidery a hobby of the past, and her
sister suggested she switch to painting. Her folksy canvases
of the quieter, gentler New England of her childhood sold for
thousands of dollars—a princely sum in the 1930s. Presidents
Harry S. Truman and John F. Kennedy lauded the little lady,
and a 1950 documentary about her life received an Oscar nod.
Despite the accolades, she retained her modesty. She wrote
in her autobiography, "I look back on my life like a good day's
work. It was done, and I feel satisfied with it."

Born in the Big Woods of Wisconsin, Laura Ingalls Wilder
taught in a one-room prairie schoolhouse, and she felt that
was to serve as her legacy until, at age sixty-five, her daughter
convinced her to pen her memories of growing up with Pa,
Ma, and her sisters on the American frontier. *The Little House
on the Prairie* led to a nine-book series that's never been out of
print, and though she could never have imagined it, an iconic
television series replete with Hollywood stars.

Is everything you cook devoid of taste? Do not despair.
Julia Child was thirty-seven before she enrolled in culinary
school and forty-nine when she published her classic,
Mastering the Art of French Cooking. She gained further acclaim
at age fifty-one as the host of *The French Chef,* where she
signed off each segment with "*Bon appétit!*"

Ageism coupled with misogyny came into play when
the sixty-eight-year-old Hillary Clinton made a play for the
Oval Office, although the mindset of many was that a lady
of a certain age is generally rendered invisible. Maybe a wise
grandfather made sense, but a grandma? Ruling the roost of

the White House? Did. Not. Sit. Well. One voter described her to *The Washington Post* as "an angry, crotchety old hag." The election proved that America is not a country for old women. The gender stereotype is alive and kicking because, although we worship youthful femininity and idolize good ole' Mom, we fall short when women do not fit into either of these roles. Being forced into silence is as palpable as a physical blow, but that has happened to marginalized seniors. What about all their wisdom, experience, and insights? Females—along with killer whales, the only other species to go through menopause—have passed through the rite of reproduction and have come to a time in their lives when they should be able to shepherd the younger generation. Thankfully, there exists what stayed in Pandora's box: hope. At age eighty-five, Supreme Court Justice Ruth Bader Ginsburg is so respected that she received a street name: Notorious R. B. G. The former head of the Federal Reserve, Chairman Janet L. Yellen, seventy-one, and the International Monetary Fund Chief, Christine Lagarde, sixty-two, prove ladies know more about money than how to spend it. The time to shed the garment of invisibility has arrived. Lives well-lived help shatter the mindset that older gals either are off their rocker or belong on one.

It may be an eye-opener to learn that one who praised older women was Benjamin Franklin; the Founding Father was actually into the Founding Mothers. When he wasn't busy wiping his bifocals (which he invented) or flying a kite in a rainstorm, our nation's first Postmaster wrote a letter to a young friend, advising, "In all your Amours you should prefer old women to young ones." In the letter, never mailed though likely shared in ye olde locker-room, Ben suggests it's best to wed and bed matrons rather than virgins, "Because when women cease to be handsome, they study to be good. Because there is no hazard of children. Because they are so grateful."

Rather than viewing wrinkles as a mark of shame, ladies of a certain age should embrace their lines—testimony to laughter, love, and life. They should not stress if they did not merit a mention in *Forbes*'s Under-Thirty list or see their names on the best-seller lists. Hope must spring eternal: There is still time to pursue dormant dreams and to wallow in the joy of proving the naysayers wrong. Keeping this thought in my mind, *Great Second Acts: In Praise of Older Women* is my seventh book. While I am in my sixth decade, I still harbor hope that one day I will publish a novel—my dream-the-impossible-dream. My philosophy, engraved on my necklace by jewelry designer Emily Rosenfeld, reads, "Make room for what is yet to be imagined."

The lives of the ladies profiled remind anyone who shrugs off the idea of great second acts of the mantra "never say never," that the silver-haired can actualize their aspirations in their golden years. In the words of Robert Browning, "Grow old with me/ The best is yet to be/ The last of life, for which the first was made..."

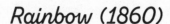

CHAPTER ONE

Rainbow (1860)

Whether Ms. Moses found the sobriquet "Grandma" a term of endearment or an unwelcome reminder of the onslaught of time is a matter of conjecture, but in either contingency, she was inextricably bound with the name. Her life, one supposed to be exempt from Warhol's fifteen minutes of fame, was as fanciful as her canvases. Her biography serves as a testament that one can receive a late-night knock at the door from the hand of fate.

Anna Mary was born in Greenwich, New York, to a frugal farming family. One of five daughters and five sons of Russell King Robertson and Margaret nee Shanahan, Anna took immense pride that one of her great-grandfathers fought in the American Revolution and had left a powder horn with the inscription, "Hezekiah King. Ticonderoga. Feb. 24th 1777 Steal not this horn for fear of shame / For on it is the owner's name." As a child, she discovered the beauty of nature when her father took his children for walks, an activity he felt brought them closer to God than services at the Methodist church. What little formal education she received was from a teacher in a one-room country school. She recalled that girls did not often go to school in winter, due to the cold and inadequate clothing, and consequently, many only progressed through the "Sixth Reader." Her favorite pastime was to color paper dolls with a tint she made from the juice of grapes and lemons. Her first experience with actual paint was when her father refurbished their farmhouse and shared the leftover paint. The precious product enabled her to create what she mispronounced as "lamb-scapes." Mr. Robertson was encouraging, but her mother thought she should spend her time in other ways. Those other ways involved household chores such as making candles, soaps, and dresses—skills she would need in a job as a hired girl.

At age twelve, her parents sent her to work as a maid at a larger farm where she met, and fifteen years later married, her employer's hired hand, Thomas Salmon Moses. She said her husband was "a wonderful man, much better than I am." With $600 in savings, the young couple rented a farm in the Shenandoah Valley of Virginia. Anna bore ten children and raised the five who survived childbirth. She supplemented the family income by making butter and potato chips (a novelty in those times) to sell to neighbors. After eighteen years in the South, the Moses family moved north again to Eagle Bridge, New York, where they bought a dairy farm. The children married and had large families; the grandchildren helped alleviate the passing of an adult daughter and the loss of Thomas that left Anna a sixty-seven-year-old widow. With the assistance of son Forrest, she managed to keep her home. To distract herself, she turned to embroidery and "worsted pictures," but this hobby ended when she developed debilitating arthritis. Her sister Celestia, remembering how she had loved to paint as a child, suggested a return to her first passion. Anna Mary agreed; she could no longer hold a needle, but she could handle a brush, and she had been too industrious all her life to be idle. She recalled, "I painted for pleasure, to keep busy, and to pass the time away, but I thought no more of it than of doing fancy work." Looking out the window of her home onto corn and tomato fields that stretched to the Hoosier River, Anna, propped on pillows, sat in a battered swivel chair. Foregoing an easel, she painted on a canvas that rested on her old kitchen table that held jam jars filled with paint. In her "studio" was an electric washer and dryer. In 1935, at age seventy-six, Anna Mary's career was born. The local county fair organizers finally persuaded Ms. Moses to send some of her pictures to exhibit, and she complied, bringing along her canned fruits and jams to sell. While her preserves won prizes, her canvases attracted scant attention. In the nearby town of Hoosick Falls, the owner of a drugstore placed some of her pictures in its window-priced from $3.00 to $5.00, based on size—alongside jars of jam, a gesture that helped soothe her ego. The brightly colored canvases attracted the attention of Louis Caldor, a New York art collector, who bought them all, then drove to the artist's home and purchased her ten remaining paintings. In the city, he tried to interest gallery owners in the elderly, rural artist; however, they did not share his enthusiasm and shrugged them off as "primitive."

Two years later, Caldor presented Anna's work to Otto Kallir, owner of the Galerie St. Etienne, who had introduced the work of Gustav Klimt to the United States. In 1928, Kallir had been one of Vienna's most prominent Jewish art dealers who found himself arranging the sale of a painting to history's most sinister art lover: Adolf Hitler. The dictator wanted *Portrait of a Young Lady* by Ferdinand Georg Waldmüller, and Kallir was the unwilling middleman. Denying the Führer a coveted painting would have been a fatal mistake. Although the heavy eroticism of Klimt was far afield from the pastoral Americana of Moses, Otto took on Anna as his client. He believed that a public mired in the Great Depression and fearful of the rumblings of a World War would embrace a world of innocence. Grandma Moses did all of her painting from her remembrance of things past. In *Wash Day*, newly laundered garments flap in the wind so vividly one can almost smell their crispness. The shape of each shirt and towel makes the canvas resemble a patchwork quilt. Even the depiction of a threatening blizzard that causes hats to fly away, branches to bend against the onslaught of the wind, fails to elicit a sense of doom. Anna tinged her canvasses with the nostalgia of Thanksgiving preparations, the pristine beauty of a snowfall, the arrival of spring, a pigmented, pragmatic poetry. They were as cheery, nostalgic, and commonsensical as Grandma herself. She said, "I like to paint old-timey things—something real pretty. Most of them are daydreams, as it were."

Under Kallir's patronage, Anna became an American idol. Her first one-woman show, in 1940, had a title that would precipitate a feminist uproar today: "What a Farm Wife Painted" proved a runaway success. However, the artist, who had recently celebrated her eightieth birthday, was a no-show. She explained that October was a busy month on the farm, and, besides, she had already seen the pictures. In a review of the exhibition, the *New York Herald Tribune* noted that the elderly artist was known locally as "Grandma Moses," and the name stuck. When Anna finally consented to come to New York in November for a Thanksgiving festival featuring her work at Gimbels Department Store, she drew a sizeable crowd who gathered to hear her talk about technique. Instead, she spoke about how she made preserves and concluded by opening her handbag and showing a few samples. The jaded urban public was delighted. She captured the craze for quaint, and the little lady became big business. Kallir brokered a lucrative deal with Hallmark Corporation to have her images reproduced, and they appeared on sixteen million Grandma Moses Christmas cards in 1947, along with reproductions that graced aprons, dishes, and lampshades. The following year, the cards debuted in Vienna and in fifteen other European cities. Merchandisers used her name to push everything from Wheaties to Old Golds. Behind the blitz was Otto, a master marketer, and the artist became an octogenarian photo-op queen. Dressed in old-fashioned clothes, hair pulled into a no nonsense bun, she posed with movie stars and politicians and appeared on a television show with Edward R. Murrow, where she demonstrated her artistry. Norman Rockwell, a younger practitioner of Americana, became a friend. Anna appeared on the far-left edge in his painting *Christmas Homecoming*, which served as the *Saturday Evening Post's* 1948 holiday cover. The zeitgeist of America preferred authentic subjects, as opposed to abstract paintings, and the public lionized the little lady. Anna earned a further niche in pop culture when Granny Clampett of the Beverly Hillbillies was given the name Daisy Moses in homage. Devotees compared Moses to the great self-taught French painter Henri Rousseau, as well as to Breughel. Until the comparisons, she had never heard of either.

Further fame arrived in 1939, when Anna had a private showing of her works at the Museum of Modern Art. During World War II, she became a patriotic darling, and as Bing Crosby sang "White Christmas," she painted *White Christmas.* As a goodwill gesture during the Cold War, the United States Government sent fifty of her paintings to Europe. At this juncture, her work had appeared in more than 160 exhibitions, and she had the only *Ecole Americaine* picture hanging in Paris's Museum of Modern Art. The artist, patron saint of small-town life, stayed at home. Other honors arrived when Russell Sage College made her an honorary doctor of humane letters. Her concern was, "They didn't let me keep the cap." After President Truman presented her with an award, she stated, "I talked with him, and I could not think but that he was one of my own boys." General Eisenhower's card from Europe manifested his admiration, "For Grandma Moses, a real artist, from a rank amateur." In 1952, Lillian Gish portrayed Moses on a televised docudrama based on her autobiography, *My Life's History.* One can only imagine Anna's emotion when she appeared on the cover of *TIME* magazine in 1953 at age ninety-three, dressed in a black dress and white lace collar.

Even as the years piled up, Anna refused to let age put the brakes on her spirit, and she produced three or four paintings every week. She said she only stopped when she became too tired— "Then I leave it to do something else; when my hand gets tired, it isn't so stiddy." When she allowed herself to rest, she watched television Westerns, not for the drama, but because of the horses. Her great fame at an advanced age pleased her because of the people she met, though it troubled her when their numbers proved daunting. A "Do Not Disturb" sign from a hotel room hung outside her front door to ward off the thousands of tourists who besieged the

Moses' homestead. A visitor who got past the printed plaque asked her of what she was most proud, and the answer could not have been more Christian, or more grandmotherly: "I've helped some people." As she wrote at a time when she was enduring infirmity and had outlived all but two of her children, "It was foolish to sleep when there is so much to do all over."

Ms. Moses passed away in 1961, at age 101, survived by nine grandchildren and more than thirty great-grandchildren. As with most artists, posthumously, her paintings increased in value. In 2006, her *Sugaring Off* sold for $1.2 million; in 1969, a six-cent US postage stamp bore the image of her painting *Fourth of July*; the original resides in the White House. President Kennedy paid her tribute and said Americans mourned the loss of the artist who had restored a primitive perception of the country's past. However, the most fitting epitaph came from her autobiography, "I look back on my life like a good day's work, it was done, and I feel satisfied with it. I was happy and contented, I knew nothing better and made the best out of what life offered. And life is what we make it, always has been, always will be."

While naysayers criticized Anna's creations as primitive, this quality held the key to her timeless appeal. It was a secret Pablo Picasso had understood: "It took me four years to paint like Raphael, but a lifetime to paint like a child." Grandma's final work, created just before her death, was aptly entitled *Rainbow*.

CHAPTER TWO

Know It Was Not Easy (1894)

When we think of an activist, the image that might come to mind is of an emaciated man marching to the sea in India, a Buddhist monk immolating himself in Vietnam, an athlete with an upraised fist in Mexico City. No one would envision a radical as a toothless woman who spoke in black Southern dialect. Despite her nickname and ancient appearance, she emanated a vivacity that makes "Moms" forever young.

Dorothy Parker hid heartache behind a wisecrack, and that was the stock in trade of Loretta Mary Aiken. Although she spent seven decades making people laugh, her own life had more than its share of grief. Loretta was the great-granddaughter of slaves and grew up in conditions scarcely better. Aiken, from rural North Carolina, was one of sixteen children, raised in poverty and segregation. At age eleven, she was raped by an older black man, a traumatic event repeated two years later by the town's white sheriff. The molestations resulted in pregnancies and the removal of the babies at birth. Shortly afterward, against her wishes, she married an older man whom she despised; she eventually bore a daughter who became a drug addict. Further events also made her life the stuff of Greek tragedy: Loretta's father, James, died in an explosion of the fire truck in which he was a passenger, and a mail truck ran over and killed her mother, Mary, as she was returning home from church on Christmas Day. At the age of fourteen, Loretta ran away and ended up in Cleveland, where she pursued a job in entertainment, hoping to find an escape from grimmer-than-is-bearable reality. She joined the Theatre Owners Booking Association—the only venue where blacks could perform during the reign of Jim Crow—colloquially known as the Chitlin Circuit. It derived its name after chitterlings, the soul food staple consisting of cooked pig intestines. Fellow performer Jack Mabley was her boyfriend for a brief period, and she adopted the name Jackie Mabley. Later, she quipped that he had taken so much from her that it was only fitting she take something from him. Mabley, in alchemist fashion, turned the base metal of tragedy into comic gold. Arsenio Hall explained this formula when he stated, "If pain makes you funny, we definitely know why Mabley was hilarious." Moms Mabley became the Southern version of the Italian crying clown who masked his tears through laughter.

Jackie's professional alter ego, the origin of her stage name, Moms Mabley, was based on her grandmother, the sole ray of light and love from her Dickensian childhood. In the 1920s, Mabley was the only female standup comedian in the world, three decades before Lucille Ball, Joan Rivers, and Phyllis Diller became known as trailblazers. Her shtick involved dressing in geriatric couture—ratty housecoat, floppy shoes, knit hats—and letting loose about whatever she damn well pleased. Dressing as a senior citizen proved convenient, as popular opinion holds the elderly are immune to the verbal censor. Moving her jaw back and forth to emulate a toothless crone, she resorted to self-mockery with her routine, "How you like Mom's dress? You know you can get some real nice things with them Green Stamps." Life had bruised the comic, but she refused to let the bruise define her.

On stage Moms was a "dirty old lady," the original cougar, with a penchant for young men. She poked fun at older men, subtly ridiculing the way they wielded authority over women as well as the decline of their sexual prowess. Her signature lines were, "Ain't nothin' an old man can do for me but bring me a message from a young one. Only time you see me with my arms around some old man, I'm holding him for the police." Moms said, about her wedding to a man nearing his dotage, "He was a man so old and weak that at their wedding somebody threw one grain of rice and it knocked him out." The comedienne's material mined the topic of sex, and her humor—scandalous in the context of the era—revolved around the risqué double-entendre.

Off stage, the ridiculously patterned housedress disappeared, and it became apparent why she had traded the name Loretta for Jackie. Private photographs depict her as she was away from the public eye: a lesbian with slicked-back hair, dapper men's suits, gambling with the boys. While onstage she played the "dog" longing to rub up against Cab Calloway, offstage, her hands rested on showgirls' knees. Norma Miller, a dancer on the circuit, recalled, "She and I shared a dressing room for two weeks—she and I and her girlfriend. We never called Moms homosexual. The word never fit her. We never called her gay. We called her Mr. Moms." Jackie never revealed this side to her audience and provided only veiled autobiographical tidbits in a gravelly voice, one that could make a tax return seem humorous. But under the surface lay an undercurrent of depth, apparent when she stated, "Don't let my looks fool you. I've been where the wild goose went." One can understand Moms' reticence in keeping mum about her sexual preference. Even seventy years later, when Ellen DeGeneres came out, the court of public opinion branded her DeGeneres the Degenerate, and sponsors pulled the plug on her eponymous show. Despite performing in the cocoon of the Chitlin Circuit, touring with Pigmeat Markam, Cootie Williams, and Bill "Bojangles" Robinson, Moms still encountered racism. It would not have behooved her to have added overt homosexuality to the mix.

Jackie provided laughter to blacks, victims of systematic racism, and in her mid-forties graduated from the Chitlin Circuit to the legendary African-American theaters in New York, the epicenter of the Harlem Renaissance. In 1939, Mabley was the first female to perform in the Apollo Theater and was a mainstay at the Cotton Club, where she provided the opening act for Duke Ellington, Count Basie, and Cab Calloway. A workaholic, she performed five shows a day, six days a week. Yet she did take time off to unwind. In the 1940s, a gay party, one the police raided for indecency.

By the 1960s, Moms had grown into her part, but even in her sixth decade, she had no intention of slowing down. She continued to have no shame—and no teeth—and thus did not need to emulate a slack jaw. In an early movie clip, she gave a member of the stage crew a Herculean task with the words, "Make me look like Lena Horne, if you possibly can, Mr. Light Man." In her outlandish housecoats, ill-fitting hats, and oversized shoes that made for a shuffling gait, she brought a slice of black perspective into white America's living rooms. When Mabley delivered her jokes, she did it in the most disarming manner possible: She took out her teeth and hammed it up like a sassy old lady sitting on the neighborhood stoop. What was not readily apparent was that, behind the gummy grin and the gravel voice that sounded uncannily like Louis Armstrong, lurked a savvy woman who used jokes to couch social commentary. A clip from a 1969 episode of *The Merv Griffin Show* profiles Moms in a psychedelic housecoat, telling a story about the special name she was called in the South.

"What's that man got that horse in pictures..that Western man?" Mabley asked Griffin.

"Roy Rogers?" was the reply.

"Then name me Roy Rogers' horse.."

"Trigger," Griffin suggests.

"Yeah, everywhere I go, they're, 'Hello, Trigger. What you saying, Trigger?' At least, I think that's what they say."

Griffin blanched when he realized he had been set up as the straight man. Other milestone small-screen appearances were on *The Smothers Brothers Comedy Hour, The Ed Sullivan Show,* and *The Tonight Show starring Johnny Carson.* In the latter, she sat down with knees considerably far apart. When the audience laughed, Moms responded, "It may be old, but it's clean."

More acclaim followed the woman born in an overcrowded rural shack; she became the first black female to appear on the stage at Carnegie Hall and went from making fourteen dollars a week on the Chitlin Circuit to, in her heyday, earning $10,000 a week. Talented both on and off the stage, Jackie wrote a musical with Zora Neale Hurston. The career she had mined from the pain of her youth provided the means to enjoy a chauffeur-driven Rolls-Royce, a sable coat, and a place in history as a show business pioneer. Despite her celebrity status and elevated economic means, she never put on airs. For ten consecutive years, she visited Sing Sing Correctional Facility on Christmas Eve and performed for the inmates, who she referred to as "Moms' children." Her jokes about the wardens made her a favorite with men who had little to laugh about.

In 1972, at age seventy-eight, Mabley made an appearance at the Kennedy Center, where she began her routine with a fictional phone conversation with President Johnson by barking, "What you want, boy?" and then sang a lullaby with a verse about "muggin' time up North." Although she never met L. B. J., she did meet President Kennedy when he invited her to the White House. She was also an acquaintance of Dr. Martin Luther King, Jr. Her bond with two giants of the twentieth century gave poignancy to her song, "Abraham, Martin, and John." Her rendition hit the US Top 40, making Mabley, then seventy-five, the oldest person to have a Top 40 hit. At age eighty-one, Moms starred for the first time in a movie, aptly titled—given the trajectory of her life—*Amazing Grace*. Her character was a rabble-rousing community agitator. Jackie suffered a heart attack midway through the film, but as soon as she received a pacemaker, she returned to the set. After filming, she set about planning future club dates. The entertainer who performed the spectrum from a correctional facility to the White House was always ready to go anywhere, at any time, with one exception. Moms stated, "There was some horrible things done to me. I've played every state in the Union—except Mississippi. I won't go there. They ain't ready."

Whoopi Goldberg decided to make a documentary about the Clown Princess of Comedy to rescue Mabley from being a mere footnote in entertainment history, despite the fact that she had paved the way for minority and women performers. The result was HBO's *Whoopi Goldberg Presents Moms Mabley*. Ms. Goldberg depicted her heroine's story through rare live footage of some of her performances, photographs, and interviews with actors, including Harry Belafonte, Bill Cosby, Kathy Griffin, Arsenio Hall, Sidney Poitier, and Jerry Stiller. Eddie Murphy based the grandmotherly character in *The Nutty Professor* on Moms. Joan Rivers, a graduate of Mabley's school of satire, was another to sing the late great's praises with the tribute, "She's been lost somewhere in comedic history." Always one to give credit where credit was due, Moms said, "Every comedian has stolen from me but Redd Foxx. He's a born comedian."

The angels were in need of laughter, and in 1975, Mabley joined their celestial number when she passed away in White Plains, New York. Clarice Taylor, who played Anna Huxtable, actor Bill Cosby's mother on *The Cosby Show*, said of the comedienne's life, "Know it was not easy."

CHAPTER THREE

The Female of the Species (1898)

In some instances, a single name is closely associated with a country: Cleopatra with ancient Egypt, Marie Antoinette with France, Victoria with England. The same situation holds true for a nation born in the twentieth century that will forever be associated with a force of nature who refused to be defined by her sex or by her age.

A stranger-than-fiction life began with Golda Mabovitch, born in Kiev, in the Russian Empire. Her first memory was of her father, Moshe, nailing boards over the front door during rumors of an imminent pogrom. In addition to the anti-Semitism, the family suffered from poverty: Her parents sometimes gave her food to her younger sister Zipke; her older sister Sheyna often fainted from hunger. Golda remembered, "I was always a little too cold outside and a little too empty inside."

In 1906, the family immigrated to the United States, where Mr. Mabovitch spent three years saving for *shifskarte* (the steamship fare.) When he could find employment, he worked as a carpenter; his wife started a dairy store, the bane of Golda's life. At age eight, Golda had to work there while her mother bought supplies at the market. Humiliated, she arrived late to school every morning.

At age eleven, to raise money for classroom textbooks, Golda organized her first public meeting and delivered her first public speech. A few years later, mother Bluma and daughter Golda got into a terrible fight when Golda announced she wanted to become a teacher. This decision did not sit well with her parents, as a Wisconsin law did not allow teachers to be married, and they feared their daughter's destiny would be that of an old maid. Desperate not to become the wife of Mr. Goodman, who was twice her age, the fourteen-year-old fled to Denver, where Sheyna—a fiery revolutionary—lived. Listening to the young socialists who congregated at her sister's home solidified her belief in Zionism. After a sibling argument, the sixteen-year-old Golda moved in with friends and started at a job measuring skirt linings. In later years, she found herself habitually glancing at hems. Her father poured on the guilt when he wrote that, if she valued her mother's life, she would return to Milwaukee. The prodigal daughter returned home, where she worked in her choice of profession. After she heard of attacks on Jews in the Ukraine and Poland, Golda organized a protest march. She turned the Mabovitch home into a mecca for visitors from Palestine. She recalled, "I knew that I was not going to be a parlor Zionist."

In 1917, Miss Mabovitch met Morris Myerson, a poetry-loving sign painter and fellow émigré from Russia. They started dating, although they had little in common other than a mutual love of classical music. At age nineteen, when Morris agreed to be part of the third *aliyah* (wave of immigration to Palestine), Golda became Mrs. Myerson. In 1921, the couple sailed on the *Pocahontas* to their second adopted country.

The newlyweds settled in Tel Aviv and joined the Kibbutz Merhavia, whose name translates to "God's wide spaces," situated a few miles south of Nazareth. The members of the commune grudgingly accepted them, and Golda felt they only agreed because of her phonograph and records. Following disagreements with the other members, she realized Merhavia would gladly have "accepted the dowry without the bride." Golda raised chickens, worked the land, and studied Hebrew, a language she had never felt comfortable conversing. Regarding her new homeland, she echoed her compatriots' complaint against Moses, saying, "He dragged us forty years through the desert to bring us to the one place in the Middle East where there was no oil." Although the kibbutz was in a malaria-ridden area and the work difficult, she embraced her new country. The frail Morris did not share her enthusiasm, and they moved to Jerusalem, where she gave birth to son, Menachem, and daughter, Sarah. Golda admitted that the four years they stayed in the capital were grueling, as the family could barely subsist on Morris's income as a bookkeeper. Mrs. Myerson did laundry in exchange for Menachem's tuition. In 1928, Golda, driven to work outside the confines of home, became the secretary of the women's labor council of Histadrut, supervising the vocational training of immigrant girls. She put in such long hours that Menachem and Sarah were happy when their mother had one of her regular migraine headaches, as it meant she would be home. Golda's less-than-maternal nature manifested itself when she later insisted that one of her grandchildren, born with mild Down syndrome, be sent to an institution.

Golda had accepted her position knowing that it meant frequent travel, and that her absences would put a strain on her marriage that was already on the rocks. Not willing to live a lie, with son and daughter in tow, she moved to a tiny apartment and slept on the living-room couch. When not making speeches, working as a laundress, or looking after her family, Golda embarked on affairs, sometimes juggling two lovers at once. The Myersons were still officially married when Morris died six years later. Until the day she passed away, Golda kept a photograph of herself and her husband on her night table.

Despite Golda's lasting affection for her husband and her passion for her romantic liaisons, her greatest love affair was for her spiritual homeland. After the United Nations Special Committee on Palestine approved the establishment of a Jewish state, the Arab states refused to accept the decision. The Jews realized war was imminent and that they would need arms and money. Golda—few now bothered to use Meir—left for America and returned with $50 million. David Ben-Gurion, the Prime Minister of Israel, remarked, "She was the Jewish woman who got the money which made the state possible." Part of her success stemmed from her powerful oratory. As Golda spoke, her diminutive stature receded, and her audience was left with the image of an imposing woman who radiated strength. When she became Prime Minister of the country she had helped birth and spoke in front of thousands, it seemed she was talking in her living room to a gathering of intimates.

On her return, she undertook the diplomatic, political negotiations with King Abdullah of Transjordan. Disguising herself as an Arab woman, she travelled to Amman to urge him to keep his promise to her not to join other Arab leaders in an attack. He asked her not to hurry the proclamation of a state. "We have been waiting for two thousand years," she replied. "Is that hurrying?" On May 14, 1948, she was one of twenty-five signers of Israel's independence, a woman among Israel's founding fathers. Golda remembered that, after affixing her signature to the document, she wept. By May 15, Israel was under attack by Egypt, Syria, Lebanon, Transjordan, and Iraq. The fifty-year-old Golda showed her mettle when she dug in her orthopedic heels. Bearing what was in effect Israel's first passport, Mrs. Meir returned to the United States to raise more money. Implacable in her condemnation of those who threatened the existence of Israel, she espoused her contempt: "The Arabs have become so rich they can buy anything—even anti-Semitism."

Bitten by the political bug, Golda became Minister of Labor; when asked if she felt handicapped at being a woman minister, she replied, "I don't know. I've never tried to be a man." She continued in this position until 1956, when she became Foreign Minister and served under Prime Minister Ben-Gurion. A man of strong ideas—he was the one who had prevailed on Golda Myerson to change her name to the Hebrew equivalent Meir—called her the only man in his Cabinet. In this capacity, she put in eighteen-hour days; she was what the Israelis call a *bitzuist*—a doer. In 1969, the Labor

Party selected her as its candidate for Prime Minister. That was not exactly the retirement she had in mind. She said, "Being seventy is not a sin. It's not a joy either." The Party's decision sent seismic shock waves throughout the country. She looked like a chain-smoking grandmother with a gray bun, stout frame, and Midwestern accent. Golda accepted the nomination, thereby traversing the improbable road from pogrom to Prime Minister. Golda had need of perseverance, as her tenure coincided with the Palestinian movement embracing terrorism, hijacking planes, and murdering Olympic athletes.

In 1973, Meir was upset when she did not hear from the Vatican about her plea to help broker peace; this silence was not surprising, as His Holiness had never recognized the legitimacy of Israel. Undaunted, Golda flew to meet Pope Paul VI. "Before we went to the audience," she recalled, "I said to our people: 'Listen, what's going on here?' Me, the daughter of Moshe Mabovitch, the carpenter, going to meet the Pope of the Catholics?' So, one of our people said to me, 'Just a moment, Golda, carpentry is a very respectable profession around here.'" After the head of the Church told her the Jews should be more merciful to the Palestinians, Golda responded, "Your Holiness, do you know what my earliest memory is? A pogrom in Kiev. When we were merciful and when we had no homeland and when we were weak, we were led to the gas chambers." Of the historic meeting, Golda recalled that there were moments of tension. No doubt. She stated of her interior turmoil, "I felt that I was saying what I was saying to the man of the cross, who heads the church whose symbol is the cross, under which Jews were killed for generations..." Meir's position knew no gray area; the situation boiled down to them or us. Her hardline stance was that, after the Diaspora, the Inquisition, the pogroms, and the Holocaust, the world owed the Jews their ancestral homeland.

In 1974, at age seventy-six, Mrs. Meir relinquished the reins of government to Yitzhak Rubin, telling her party she no longer had the stamina to carry the heavy mantle of leadership. Surprisingly, towards the end of her life, the powerhouse revealed she was still nursing guilt about the years during which she had neglected her children in her drive to be a mother to her nation. Her mea culpa: "There is a type of woman who does not let her husband narrow her horizons. Despite the place her children and family fill in her life, her nature demands something more; she cannot divorce herself from the larger social life. For such a woman there is no rest."

Rest finally came for Golda in 1978 when she passed away in Jerusalem's Hadassah Hospital at age eighty. In announcing her death, hospital officials disclosed one of Israel's best-kept secrets; she had been suffering from cancer since the late 1960s, as she was leading Israel through its 1973 war. Ms. Meir did not permit disclosure of her illness, even at the end. Ironically, death came for Golda with Israel on the brink of peace with Egypt, a goal she had sought for almost six decades of Sisyphean struggle. In 1974, she said, "Someday, peace will come, but I doubt that I will still be here to see it." However, Golda came closer to realizing her dream than she had expected. In honor of her selfless devotion, the government laid their own iron lady to rest near the visionary of Zionism, Theodor Herzl.

Golda had always downplayed her femininity, perhaps a necessary tactic to scale the ranks in a patriarchy. And yet she was at her core a mother lion who proved the truth of Kipling's words, "The female of the species is more deadly than the male."

CHAPTER FOUR

On and On (1893)

For Oscar Wilde, the one unforgivable sin was to be boring. "Dull" was never an adjective that society could pin on a centenarian ceramist. She lived and loved in her own way, and served as inspiration for one of film's most iconic characters.

Beatrice Wood was born in San Francisco; when she was five, her family relocated to New York, to an exclusive zip code on the Upper East Side. Her mother's main parental concern was preparation for her daughter's debut to Manhattan society, which entailed a year in a convent school in Paris, enrollment in a finishing school, and summer trips to Europe to visit art galleries, museums, and theaters. Ironically, this exposure to the arts sabotaged Mrs. Wood's vision of Beatrice following in her well-heeled footsteps. In 1912, the teen spurned the idea of becoming a trophy wife and dreamed of a future as a painter. Realizing the futility of argument, her mother sent her—nanny in tow—to France to study at the Académie Julian. Finding the curriculum tedious, Beatrice ran away from her chaperone and moved into an attic room. Never short on nerve, she peered through a hedge to watch Claude Monet painting amidst his flowerbeds. She moved to Paris, where she turned her attention to the theater, enrolled in the Comédie-Française, and shared the stage with Sarah Bernhardt.

With the storm clouds of World War I hovering, the Woods insisted that Beatrice return home, and to their chagrin, they were unable to dissuade her from a career as an actress. Bilingual and beautiful, she obtained a position in the French National Repertory Theatre under the stage name Mademoiselle Patricia, a necessary move as acting was not a reputable profession for a girl from the right side of the

tracks. During her tenure, she rubbed shoulders with fellow
thespians; she shared a dressing room with the poet Edna
St. Vincent Millay and knitted a scarf for Isadora Duncan.
Beatrice was grateful for her work, as she wanted money to
escape her home where "I was a good little girl. Nothing is
more revolting."

After performances, she hung out with the most
adventurous artistic characters in town, such as Man Ray
and film star Myrna Loy. When informed that Edgard Varèse,
a French vanguard composer, was in a hospital with a
broken leg, she paid him a visit. Through him she met Henri-
Pierre Roché, a diplomat and writer, who became her first
lover, and who broke her heart. The problem was that she
"was a monogamist woman in a polygamous world." After
their breakup, she fell for Marcel Duchamp, best known for
Nude Descending a Staircase. He was an integral part of the
Dada movement, an avant-garde trend that traditionalists
considered blasphemy. Its adherents found patrons in the
stratospherically wealthy Walter and Louise Arensberg—the
first American collectors of modern art—who held evening
soirées at their luxurious duplex apartment. Duchamp served
as their star attraction; other guests were Beatrice Woods,
Isadora Duncan, and William Carlos Williams.

A 1917 photograph shows Duchamp and Wood at Coney
Island; Beatrice is seated on a fake ox, while behind her, in
an oxcart, against a painted background, her lover is perched.
Beatrice reminisced, "With Marcel's arm around me, I would
have gone on any ride into hell with the same heroic abandon
as a Japanese lover standing on the rim of a volcano, ready to
take a suicide leap." Duchamp gave Wood her initial push into
the world of modern art. After her remark that "anyone can
do such scrawls," he dared her to try. Impressed with *Marriage
of a Friend*, he submitted it to *Rogue* magazine. Their romance
ended when his relationship mantra echoed Henri-Pierre's:
lust can be divorced from love.

Roché, Duchamp, and Wood organized the Society of Independent Artists and published the avant garde journal *The Blind Man*, leading to Beatrice's moniker, the Mama of Dada. Her life attracted attention when Roché's novel about an *amour a trois, Jules and Jim*, inspired Francois Truffaut's 1961 movie of the same name, where actress Jeanne Moreau played the role of Ms. Wood. Beatrice denied its verisimilitude, claiming she was a serial monogamist. Despite numerous heartbreaks, she held steadfast to romantic illusions. As she told an interviewer, "If a man says he loves me, I fall into his lap like a ripe grape."

In 1918, fed up with her mother's meddling in her on and off stage life, Beatrice ran away to Montreal, Canada, with her friend Paul, a theater manager. He convinced her the way to achieve autonomy from family was to marry him, which she did at age twenty-five. They shared a marriage of convenience, mostly for hubby, who used his wife's earnings to support his gambling habit. The union was declared void when it was discovered that he already had a wife in Belgium. After the divorce, Beatrice rarely spoke of Paul, and identified him only by his first name. Beatrice returned to the Big Apple; however, the worm in its core was the fact that the Dada movement had died down, Marcel was traveling in Europe, and Roché had returned to Paris. Theater also had lost its lure; as an art form, it remained fascinating, but she disliked the role of actress because "You become so concentrated on yourself, your smile, and the way you look. And, really, it's a pain in the ass." In 1938, after another love, the British director Reginald Pole, left her to marry an eighteen-year-old, she moved to California to be near the Indian guru Krishnamurti, of whom she had become a disciple. The move segued into her great second act.

On a trip to Holland, Beatrice had purchased a set of baroque dessert plates with a lustrous glaze. Unable to find a matching teapot, she decided to create one, and at age forty, she enrolled in a ceramics course at Hollywood High School.

Intrigued with the process, it became her new art medium, and she became the pupil of Otto Natzler, a Jewish artist who had fled his homeland when the Nazis annexed Austria. Her work—reminiscent of Dada—poked fun at social hypocrisy and the battle of the sexes, while others were heavily erotic. A favorite subject was Shakespeare's red-headed patron, and in one of her brochures for an exhibition, she wrote, "Did you know what Queen Elizabeth I did with ambassadors? Each had to spend a night with her, and the one with the best qualifications got the job." Wood also fashioned chalices and bowls, the shapes culled from Greek, Japanese, and Indian sources. Endlessly experimental, she said, "Knowing what one's about to take out of a kiln is as exciting as being married to a boring man." Anais Nin remarked that her works were "iridescent and smoky, like trail-ways left by satellites." Beatrice said of her medium, "Women who have diamonds—it can't touch the joy and excitement of opening a kiln." The ceramics supported her through the Depression (she did not inherit family money), and the Los Angeles County Museum of Art, the Metropolitan Museum of Art in New York, and upscale stores such as Neiman Marcus carried her works signed Beato, her nickname.

In 1948, taken with its purple mountains, pink-blue sunsets, and "unique aura," the bohemian Beatrice found her forever home in Ojai, California. Krishnamurti had introduced her to the area. Later, he, Beatrice, and another resident, Aldous Huxley, founded the Happy Valley School, a no-grades progressive institution in the Upper Ojai Valley, where Wood taught pottery. She also took another trip down the aisle with Steven Hoag, with whom she shared an amicable, platonic marriage that lasted for several years until his passing. The prosaic reason for their nuptial was that it allowed them to apply for Red Cross funding (married couples had a better chance) when the house they owned in North Hollywood washed away in a flood. In her autobiography, *I Shock Myself*, published when Wood was ninety-two, she wrote, "In a way my life has been an upside-down experience. I never made love to the two men I married, and I did not marry the men I loved. I do not know if this makes me a good girl gone bad, or a bad girl gone good." Beatrice's last grand passion was with an East Indian scientist with whom she fell in love at age sixty-eight, on the first of her three trips to India. She refused to name him to protect his conservative family. Wood described the affair with the mystery man who told her that "our trains move in opposite directions" in her fourth book, *33rd Wife of a Maharajah,* published in India.

Beatrice's ninth decade was her most artistic exploratory period, and her mental agility remained as sharp as ever; as a ninety-year-old, she learned to use a personal computer for her correspondence. Far from dressing her age in conservative fashion with a prim gray bun, Wood wore her hair in a long thick braid, sported a challenging amount of silver jewelry, and dressed in brightly colored saris. Her ranch-style studio home in the Topa Topa Mountain area doubled as a gallery that drew 300 visitors a month. Wood did not allow her failing health to prevent her from ever being anything other than a gracious hostess. When asked the key to her longevity, she attributed it to "art books, chocolate and young men." (Hence guests arrived with gifts of the former.) In all likelihood, her vegetarian diet and avoidance of alcohol and tobacco had something to do with the fact she appeared far younger. Beatrice explained the reason she was a teetotaler: "I don't drink because I decided long ago, if I was going to be seduced, I wanted to be sober." In her autobiography, she highlighted a life that had embraced the road less travelled; she had befriended ballet figures Nijinsky and Pavlova, the artist Brancusi, and the director Stanislavsky. The artist insisted that, since scientists had proved time and space did not exist, she was "actually only thirty-two." One fan of Camp Wood was Governor Pete Wilson of California, who deemed her "a national treasure." Another was film director James Cameron—a neighbor in Ojai—who used her as the model for the 101-year-old Rose in *Titanic,* played by Oscar nominee Gloria Stuart. Despite her acclaim, she still retained her youthful romanticism, and said with a sly smile, "I still would be willing to sell my soul to the devil for a nice Argentine to do the tango with."

Unlike many older people who dwell on the past, to her, the good old days were always the current ones. A premiere in Los Angeles featured a documentary on her life, *Beatrice Wood: Mama of Dada*, produced by Diandra Douglas (the ex-wife of actor Michael.) Three years later, she celebrated her 103rd birthday with a retrospective exhibition of 103 objects, many recently made, at La Jolla's Mingei International Museum of World Folk Art. Her pieces are on display in the permanent collections of twelve major museums, including the Smithsonian and the Metropolitan Museum of Art, and command prices of $40,000 per piece. When an interviewer asked why people still found her interesting, Ms. Wood replied, "I'd be interested in any old bag who was still working at age 100."

Beatrice's 105th birthday bash drew 250 guests, including James Cameron and Gloria Stewart. Ms. Wood passed away soon after, but her heart, like the celluloid Rose's, "will go on and on."

CHAPTER FIVE

Life as Theater (1896)

May-December relationships have been the fodder of the silver screen; traditionally, the former have been young women, the latter, older men. This paradigm changed with the rise of what has become known in popular parlance as the "cougar." In the movie *The Graduate*, Mrs. Robinson was Benjamin Braddock's graduation present; in *American Pie*, Stifler's mom proclaimed, "I like my scotch and men the same way—aged eighteen years"; in *Sex and the City*, Samantha Jones's boy-toy lured her down the path of monogamy. But an octogenarian was the leader of this pack of Mrs. Robinsons.

The woman who became renowned as a "cradle-robber" was Ruth Gordon Jones from Quincy, Massachusetts. Her father, Clinton, was a retired sea captain, and her mother, Annie, bartered sewing skills for her daughter's piano lessons. Ruth met her destiny at age sixteen in the upper balcony of the Colonial Theater in Boston, at a production of *The Pink Lady*. After the performance, Ruth heard voices telling her, "Go on stage!" Never one to loathe a good suggestion, she took the ethereal message to heart, and broke the news to her father that she was leaving for the Never-Never Land of Broadway. His less-than-enthusiastic response was, "What makes you think you've got the stuff?" Although the comment was harsh, the New Englander felt he was being pragmatic: his five-foot-tall daughter with bow legs was not the stuff that made for a screen siren. He advised her to become a physical education teacher, but, as Ruth said, "I wanted to do something a little more sexy than that." Armed with equal parts grit and wit, the eighteen-year-old left for New York. Clinton gave her the money for one year's tuition to the American Academy of Dramatic Arts, fifty dollars spending money, and his old spyglass from his sailor days. According to Ruth, "He told me

I could hock it if I needed money. He said if you're going to be an actress, you'll be in and out of hock shops all your life. Well, I hocked plenty of things, but never that spyglass." She loved the city and considered herself a New Yorker forever after. Although Ruth loved the city, it took time for her love to be returned. Her teachers informed her that she "showed no promise" and showed her the door. The teen refused to heed the naysayers, saying, "The will to succeed, that is half the battle. I hadn't any illusions about my ability; I only thought if other people could learn to act, I could." She wrote to her parents, "I would rather be an actress than live. In other words, if I could not be an actress I would gladly take my life. I can say that without fear because I can be an actress and will be." Despite getting the boot from her school, Ruth landed the role of one of the Lost Boys in *Peter Pan*; Alexander Woollcott wrote a review in the *New York Times* in which he denounced the supporting cast, with one exception: "Ruth Gordon was ever so gay as Nibs." Her joy was short-lived, as her mother died during the show's first week; after a brief return to Quincy, she was back at work. As a dancer in her next role, she earned $1.25 and two ham sandwiches a day. In *Seventeen*, she received a withering review when Heywood Broun wrote in the *New York Tribune*, "Anyone who looks like that and acts like that must get off the stage." She did not. A year later, she married the star of that production, Gregory Kelly. After a brief hospital stay, in which she had both her bowlegs broken and straightened (she felt it the price to pay for an aspiring star), the Kellys started a repertory company in Indianapolis. Gordon drew acclaim for a performance in *Saturday's Children*, a 1927 play costarring Humphrey Bogart. During the run, her husband's congenital heart condition worsened, and for the second time, Ruth played one drama on stage while agonizing through another offstage. She left a second-act curtain call to rush to Gregory and was with him when he died. As a widow, Ruth became romantically involved with producer Jed Harris; their romance was clandestine, as he was married. Her role as the other woman produced son Jones Harris, born in Paris.

His birth was a loosely kept secret, and they stayed in Europe for several months. As social stigma against illegitimacy lessened, Jones's life became more open, and he grew up with birthday parties at Sardi's and summers in the Catskills, where his mother toured. He eventually married a Vanderbilt.

Romantic tranquility finally arrived when Ruth married writer-director Garson Kanin in 1942; they had met briefly twice before, but the third time "was a go." Initially, she was apprehensive about their relationship because he was sixteen years her junior, but their marriage proved a triumph. The couple divided their time between a Central Park South apartment and a studio in Carnegie Hall. They were together till death did them part, and during their forty-three years of marriage, they wrote the screenplays *Pat and Mike* and *Adam's Rib*, both of which became classics for costars Spencer Tracy and Katherine Hepburn. As she approached her eightieth birthday, she told an interviewer, "Thank heaven for Garson! I wouldn't have come this far if I weren't married to the most wonderful man in the world."

Ruth's theatrical ability and trademark wit bought her entry to the Algonquin Round Table, where she lunched with fellow humorist Dorothy Parker and dined at the White House with the Franklin D. Roosevelts. Gordon also achieved acclaim on the other side of the Atlantic when she starred in *The Country Wife*, bringing the Old Vic crowd to its feet. The British critics had not believed an American could pull off such a performance, and a breathless cable from a *New York Times* correspondent read, "Last night, Ruth Gordon took London by storm!"

A film career blossomed throughout the 1940s and into the '50s. She joined Hollywood's inner circle, working and socializing with Laurence Olivier, Vivien Leigh, Merle Oberon, George Cukor, Jack Warner, and Lillian Gish. Unlike other actresses, who decided to fade away when their beauty diminished, Ruth pooh-poohed that notion. She had struggled too hard to watch her career disappear in the rearview mirror. The actress turned author when she wrote her autography; in its pages, Ruth relayed the fascinating story of how a young woman with no physical or material advantages clawed her way through the theatrical jungle of stage and screen. In *Myself Among Others*—the others are the numerous celebrities in whose orbit she travelled, such as Harpo Marx, Ethel Barrymore, Irving Berlin—she devoted several passages to reflections on aging. Ruth observed, "On my seventy-fourth birthday I dreaded looking in the glass. I didn't want any surprises, but I got one. At seventy-four, I look better than seventy-three. If you make it through seventy-four years, can it be that things shape up?" While Hollywood lore held to the paradigm that a woman can be one of two things, young or dead, Ruth did not buy into that mindset. She wrote, "Shakespeare died when he was fifty-two. If I had, I'd never have been in *The Matchmaker* or met Mia or been on *The Joey Bishop Show* or flown six times across the country or won an Oscar or eaten papaya or been robbed of all my jewelry or seen *M*A*S*H** or *Where's Poppa?* or *Don Rickles.*"

The ambitious girl from Quincy's wildest dreams came true when Roman Polanski gave her the role of Mia Farrow's devil-worshipping neighbor in *Rosemary's Baby*, which garnered the seventy-two-year-old an Academy Award for best supporting actress. Two years later, in *Where's Poppa*, she played the daffy mother who has Lucky Charms topped with Pepsi-Cola for breakfast. One of her most iconic roles was as the eighty-year-old funeral groupie who becomes the lover of a suicidal nineteen-year-old in *Harold and Maude*. While the movie's far-fetched plot pivoted on the extremity of the May-December romance, its magic emanated from the couple's mutual affection that did not allow age to impede it. Just as Harold was smitten with Maude, audiences were enamored with Ruth. No other film portrays an older woman with such dignity, as someone who is comfortable with her years, is sexually active, and is still a babe. The options for actresses of a certain age are largely roles that do not recognize their sexuality except as something that has faded—Gloria Swanson in *Sunset Boulevard*—or as carnal predators—Vivien Leigh in *A Streetcar Named Desire.* Libido does not wither at the onset of age spots. *Harold and Maude,* a movie that achieved cult status, bombed at the box office after its release. This fact is perhaps understandable, given the octogenarian leading lady and the fact that it came out the same year as *Carnal Knowledge,* starring sex kittens Candice Bergen and Ann-Margret. It took twelve years for Ruth's film to finally make a profit. Gordon said that when her $50,000 check arrived in the mail in 1983, she almost threw it away, as she mistook it for a sweepstakes offer from *Reader's Digest.*

Fifty-three years after the American Academy of Dramatic Arts dismissed Ruth from its ranks for showing no promise, the organization offered its *mea culpa.* She addressed its graduating class with the weight of many years of accumulated wisdom: "The last time I was at the Academy, the president said, 'We feel you're not suited to acting. Don't come back.' Well, you see who's standing here. And on that awful day when someone says you're not pretty, you're no good, think of me and don't give up!"

In tribute to its famous daughter, the town of Quincy held a Ruth Gordon Day and dedicated an amphitheater to her in 1984, shortly after her eighty-eighth birthday. At the ceremony, she said, "I am the first person in my family to have a theater named for her. It took a long time. I started toward this eighty-eight years, eleven days and five and a half hours ago. I never face the facts. I never listen to good advice. I'm a slow starter but I get there." Ruth was vocal about her disdain for retirement. In 1977, the eighty-one-year-old Ms. Gordon testified before the House Select Committee on Aging and said, "It's like slavery. First, you're allowed to work. Then you're not. As the great baseball player Satchel Paige once said, 'How old would you be if you didn't know how old you were?'"

At the conclusion of *Myself Among Others*, Gordon wrote of her life, "It's been awful and great and hair-raising and beautiful and side-splitting and terrifying and unbelievably groovy, and I wouldn't live over one single day of it, but will I ever hate to see that evening sun go down!" The seaman's daughter who fearlessly navigated the rocky shores of acting passed away at her Martha's Vineyard summer home with Garson at her side. He said even her last day was typically full, with walks, talks, errands, and a morning of work on a new play. She had made her last public appearance two weeks before, at a benefit showing of *Harold and Maude*, and had recently finished acting in four films. In one of them, not surprisingly, Ruth had insisted on doing her own motorcycle stunts. The obituaries claimed she was eighty-eight—a pointless statistic, as Gordon defied the constraints of age with a steely vengeance. Perhaps the best tribute can be from her own words. "I don't want to boast but I walk through New York and policemen stop and yell, 'We love you, Ruthie, we just love you...'" Out of the mouths of New York's finest. At her death, friends referred to a light going out, and in a sense, an entire theatrical galaxy had been extinguished. As Ruth once said, "If you live long enough, you are your work and your work is you." The memories of her stage performances, movies, screenplays, books, and most of all, her life as theater, live on.

CHAPTER SIX

The Only Stone Left Unturned (1905)

The 1960s was the decade when rebels had any number of causes: the Civil Rights movement, Women's Liberation, anti-Vietnam protests. There was also another battle, and though it did not make the seismic waves as did others of its era, it likewise proved a noble struggle.

One can judge a culture by how it treats its aged. Filial devotion has always been a serious business in China, deeply etched in the national psyche. At the other end of the spectrum are societies that practice senicide—the killing of the elderly. The Inuit looked at the aged as useless feeders and sent them to a watery death on an ice floe. In contemporary Western culture, unlike societies with extended family units where grandparents are integral members, the old often spend their "golden years" in retirement facilities. The atmosphere in some of these institutions reeks of disinfectant and despair. The injustice of the mistreatment of senior citizens was a wrong one woman dedicated her later years to righting.

Margaret ("Maggie") was on the road to activism before birth. In 1905, the pregnant Mrs. Kuhn was in Memphis with her husband, and unwilling to deliver a child in the segregated South, so she returned home to Buffalo before her due date. When Maggie was young, women had three career choices: teaching, nursing, or marriage; she chose none of these. As a teenager, she graduated with honors from Western Reserve University's College for Women in Cleveland, where she majored in English literature, sociology, and French. A staunch suffragette, she instituted a college chapter of the League of Women Voters. In a 1993 interview, Kuhn said her activism

began with her sociology classes that involved visits to jails,
sweatshops, and slums.

With her degree under her belt, Maggie moved to
Philadelphia and joined the Young Women's Christian
Association, where she became the head of the Department
of Business Girls. During World War II, with the men fighting
in Europe, Maggie—in Rosie the Riveter fashion—encouraged
females to exchange aprons for factory attire. The YWCA
sent her to Columbia University to study reform, and she
lectured to women workers about standing up for themselves
in a patriarchally controlled country. She found her career
niche when she became the secretary of the Social Education
and Action Department at the Presbyterian Church. In
her position, she edited the journal *Social Progress*, which
focused on the desegregation movement of the 1940s, anti-
McCarthyism in the 1950s, and ending the Vietnam War in
the 1960s.

In 1970, at age sixty-five, though she was as vital as ever,
the law mandated Maggie's resignation. Her employer gave
her a sewing machine as a parting gift, one that remained
unused. Although she had known termination was inevitable,
Ms. Kuhn recalled she felt "suddenly shocked and wounded,
then angry, at having to be sent out to pasture." Recalling
her reaction, she reflected, "Then I figured there must be
thousands of old people like me, so I decided it was time to
fight back." Political activist Ralph Nader proclaimed of the
expiration date on Maggie's career, "The most significant
retirement in modern American history." Maggie decided
she would not fade quietly away and stated, "Don't agonize,
organize." Infuriated at this injustice, she and five female
friends, whose employers had likewise been forced to cut
them loose because they were seniors, met to address the
problem of ageism in America. They formed the Consultation
of Older and Younger Adults for Social Change. The group
included the young, also victims of societal stereotyping.
In a nod to solidarity, Maggie shared her large house in

Philadelphia's Germantown neighborhood with different
generations. She referred to retirement homes as "glorified
playpens where wrinkled babies can be safe and out of the
way. There is little stimulation and people regress." If she had
to live in one, she remarked, she would just die. In a year, the
organization had more than 100,000 members in thirty-two
states and half a dozen countries. In 1972, a TV newsman
dubbed them the Gray Panthers, a spin on the name of the
civil rights group of the era. Unlike the militant group, her
choice of weapons was words. Ms. Kuhn's philosophy was,
"Speak your mind even if your voice shakes, for well-aimed
slingshots can topple giants." Maggie's mission was to end
the marginalization of the elderly, a bastion of prejudice.
As she put it, "We can no longer afford to scrap-pile people."
Headquarters was in the basement of the Tabernacle Church,
and the Gray Panthers took aim at the lack of universal
health care, economic disparity, and corporate monopolies.
Of the latter, she said, "Power should not be concentrated in
the hands of so few and powerlessness in the hands of so
many." In 1977, the group published *Nursing Homes: A Senior
Citizen's Action Guide* and initiated long-overdue legislation.
After sustained pressure from the Gray Panthers in 1986,
President Reagan, aged seventy-five, abolished the antiquated
law mandating forced retirement. Kuhn, a powerful speaker
despite her frail frame, argued, "The first myth is that old age
is a disease, a terrible disease that you never admit you've
got, so you lie about your age. Well, it's not a disease—it's a
triumph. Because you've survived. Failure, disappointment,
sickness, loss—you're still here." The Gray Panthers were
sponsors of the Black House Conference on Aging and
protested the lack of African-Americans at the first White
House Conference. Another crusade was death with dignity.
Their pro-euthanasia stance was based on the belief that
when doctors take drastic measures to keep patients alive,
they are not prolonging life; rather, they are just prolonging
death. This subject was a raw wound for Kuhn, as doctors
had kept her comatose brother alive for several days before

allowing him to pass. Maggie took steps to ensure that would never be her fate, and her lawyer, minister, and physician cosigned her living will.

In 1972, Maggie, who the *New York Times* described as a "diminutive militant," was a frail-looking woman who wore her hair in a prim bun that gave her the look of a candidate a Boy Scout would help across the street. She made no apologies for her looks or her age, saying, "I'm an old woman. I have gray hair, many wrinkles and arthritis in both hands. And I celebrate my freedom from bureaucratic restraints that once held me." In attire, matching her spirit, Maggie dressed in an unconventional manner. In a 1992 interview at her home for the *Los Angeles Times*, Kuhn sat on a sofa, petting a cat, her staid gray wool suit offset with purple tights and black Nikes. At rallies, she would show up in a minidress or a slit skirt with stylish boots. When impassioned, she would punch the air with an arthritic, clenched fist, a gesture accompanied by her organization's trademark Gray Panther Growl. Maggie told interviewers, "The human life span has almost doubled since the turn of the century. The challenge is, what are you supposed to do with that when you're supposed to retire halfway through life?" The answer was the Gray Panthers' mission.

In the 1980s, its pigment-free (gray) members went after President Reagan's budget cuts and, later, President George Bush's Gulf War. As a witness to the signing of the pension bill, President Ford called on her, asking, "What have you to say, young lady?" She felt his words were condescending, and retorted, "Mr. President, I am an *old woman.*" Maggie explained her anger by saying, "My wrinkles are a badge of distinction. I earned them. Don't flush away my life by denying them." The crown prince of television, Johnny Carson, felt her ire when she appeared on his show and criticized him for his "Aunt Blabby" routine. To make her point, she presented him with a Gray Panthers T-shirt and admonished him that the nation is full of elderly women who are not dingbats.

In her role of wearing the Gray Panther crown, her words were "honey with a hammer" as she travelled 100,000 miles a year as spokeswoman, wrote a column for the *Philadelphia Bulletin,* and authored books on aging. She was the subject of two documentary films, *Aging in America* and *Maggie Kuhn: Wrinkled Radical.* In the pages of her autobiography, entitled *No Stone Unturned: The Life and Times of Maggie Kuhn,* Maggie was as outspoken as she was in person, and her memoir included descriptions of her sexual and romantic encounters, from college days through her last decade. She expressed her romantic philosophy as, "Sex and learning end only when rigor mortis sets in." She wrote that she was fortunate to have had so many "wonderful affairs," including a fifteen-year relationship with a married minister and a liaison with a man fifty years her junior, a student at the University of Washington, begun when she was in her seventies and he was in his twenties. When asked the inevitable question as to why she had never married, Maggie's invariable response was, "Sheer luck."

In her twilight years she stated in an interview, "When I look back on my life, I see so many things I could not have done if I had been tied to a husband and children." Ms. Kuhn never attached a negative connotation to the status of "old maid." Maggie said that to deny sexuality in old age "is to deny life itself." The only time her contemporaries felt she had gone too far was her suggestion that, in late life, heterosexual women might consider lesbian relationships. This statement was in keeping with her belief that the recipe for staying alert was to "try to do at least one outrageous thing a day." Kuhn became known internationally, and by 1978, the World Almanac listed her as one of the twenty-five most influential women in the United States. In the mid 1980s, the Gray Panthers declined in membership to approximately fifty thousand, in part because of another powerful lobbying group: the American Association for Retired Persons. Ms. Kuhn said that this statistic was an indication that a new and more conservative generation of older people was to be its successor.

Despite her physical ailments—arthritis, a degenerative eye ailment, and osteoporosis, the only effects of age that she could not fight against—did not slow her down. Pleased with the inroads she had made, she reflected, "We have begun to shape and shake up an ageist society. We have begun to celebrate age, not deny it. Old age is a triumph and I think that we have made that case." Maggie survived bouts of cancer and two random street muggings that left her with a broken arm and shoulder. Two weeks before her death, she joined striking transit workers on their picket line. Although she made it her goal to live until age ninety, she felt her end was imminent and had friends celebrate her August birthdate in April. Christina Long, who helped write her autobiography, said Maggie's former lover, then in his forties, was at the celebration: "He seemed very proud of the romance." At age eighty-nine, Maggie passed away in her sleep from cardiopulmonary arrest. In her final days, wracked with pain and sedated with morphine, she sat up in bed and declared, "I am an advocate for justice and peace." Her indomitable spirit never left her, and she made good on a comment she had made years before, "I'm going to be outrageous until the end." No doubt, had she been conscious, she would have let out a last Panther roar.

Ms. Kuhn forever altered the perception of senior citizens, which, hopefully, we all will be. The firebrand of the Gray Panthers aptly summed up her life when she wrote that she would like her gravestone inscribed: "Here lies Maggie Kuhn under the only stone she left unturned."

CHAPTER SEVEN

A Nobel / Noble Woman (1909)

A battle cry of feminism—one that launched a thousand tweets, T-shirts, and tattoos—appeared in 2017, when Republican Senator Mitch McConnell shushed Elizabeth Warren. Regarding her refusal to be muzzled, he stated, "She was warned. She was given an explanation. Nevertheless, she persisted." The hashtag #LetLizSpeak began trending, along with historical examples of powerful men silencing females: Rosa Parks, Susan B. Anthony, Malala. A century earlier, a despot tried to annihilate a lady who not only persisted, but prevailed, to become a Nobel Woman.

Old habits, as has been observed, die hard and, even with the end of the Victorian era, sexism was still rampant. In the first decade of the twentieth century, Italian girls not only had to contend with misogyny, they also had to fight time-honored machismo. One who refused to conform to a sexist mold was born into an observant Jewish family in Turin. One of four children, Rita was the daughter of Adamo Levi, an electrical engineer, and Adele Montalcini, a painter, Italian Jews who could trace their roots to Israelites who immigrated during the days of the Roman Empire.

The event that altered the trajectory of Levi-Montalcini's life was the death of her governess, Giovanna, who had helped raise Rita, her twin, Paola, and her siblings, Nina and Gino. Devastated by the loss, she determined to become a doctor and find a cure for the disease that had claimed the life of her second mother. However, in the early 1900s, Italy decreed that girls' primary goals were in the domestic sphere. Because of the current zeitgeist, her parents sent their three daughters to an all-girls' high school whose graduates did not meet the criteria for acceptance into a university. This lack of education did not faze her sisters, as Paola became a painter and Nina married and became a mother of three. In contrast, Gino, free from gender restraint, became a prominent architect and professor at the University of Turin.

Rita felt she lacked her mother's and twin's artistic talent, though she had an artistic temperament, and the thought of marriage held no appeal. Indeed, she would have taken umbrage at the term "maternal instinct," as she had no desire to populate the planet. "Babies did not attract me, and I was altogether without the maternal sense so highly developed in small and adolescent girls." Although her father remained steadfast in his conviction that medical school was a man's domain, he gave his grudging approval. After intensive studying to fill the gaps in her education, Rita entered the University of Turin, one of seven women in a class of three hundred. Her professor, Giuseppe Levi (no relation), took her under his wing and helped her overcome the school's entrenched sexism, and in 1936, she graduated summa cum laude. In recognition of her achievement, Levi-Montalcini received a trip to a scientific conference in Sweden, but returned to a brutal reception.

The best-laid plans of mice and men—and an ambitious young woman—were waylaid when Benito Mussolini issued the *Manifesto per la Difesa della Razza*, signed by ten Italian scientists, that resulted in the banishment of non-Aryans from the academic and professional fields. To avoid the regime's anti-Semitism, Rita fled to Belgium, where she worked as a guest of a neurological institute. In 1940, on the eve of the Nazi invasion, she returned to Italy.

Showing that you can't keep a great woman down, Rita, with the help of her brother, converted her bedroom into a makeshift lab and filled it with the chicks she needed for research. Forced to innovate, she fashioned her own scientific instruments using, among other things, reshaped sewing needles and watchmakers' tweezers. Discovery of her clandestine activities could have resulted in imprisonment or death, but she refused to let the dictator, Il Duce, sideline her passion. After the fascists dismissed Giuseppe from his post, he ironically went to work as an assistant to his former pupil.

With the Allied bombing raining death on Turin, the Levi-Montalcini family fled to a retreat in Piemonte, where Rita set up another lab. In order to carry on her investigation of nerve growth in chicken embryos, with eggs in short supply because of wartime shortages, she bicycled around the countryside searching for fertilized ones. To deflect suspicion, she explained to the farmers that she wanted them because she felt they were more nutritious for her "babies." As a bonus, she could later turn her experiments into omelets. Forced to go on the run once more, the family escaped to Florence, where forged papers bore the surname Lupani and identified them as Catholic. In 1945, Mussolini, who fancied himself the contemporary Julius Caesar, and his mistress, Claretta Petacci, met their end through machine-gun fire. After the war, Dr. Levi-Montalcini joined the Allies as a volunteer physician in refugee camps, where she treated patients suffering from typhoid and other infectious diseases.

In 1947, Rita received a letter from Viktor Hamburger, a German-born embryologist whose writings had sparked the idea for her bedroom lab experiments. He invited her to work with him at Washington University in St. Louis, offering a month-long fellowship. Not only did she accept the post, she became a full-time Professor of Neurobiology in 1958, a position she held until her retirement at age sixty-eight. Rita never cared for the word retirement, insisting that doing so only led to the decay of the brain. During her tenure, she collaborated with Stanley Cohen, a quiet, clarinet-playing biochemist; their goal was to prove the existence of nerve growth factor (NGF). Their subsequent discovery improved the understanding of the processes involved in certain malformations, leading to treatments for diseases such as breast cancer, Alzheimer's, and senior dementia. Their findings also made progress toward the repair of damaged nerve cells. According to Pietro Calissano, who collaborated with Rita on an article for *Scientific American*, NGF may have played a role in allowing her to live until age 103. He explained that she took the serum every day in the form of eye drops. In the same publication, Rita attributed the key to her staggering success to "the absence of psychological complexes, tenacity in following the path I reputed to be right, and the habit of underestimating obstacles."

After leaving St. Louis known as "the lady of the cells," Rita returned to Italy, where she lived with Paola and maintained a much-marked appointment book. In addition to her duties as a teacher, she set up schools for female scientists and founded the Institute of Cell Biology of the Italian National Council of Research. Rita divided her time between her adopted country and the land of her birth but, regardless of *la professoressa*'s time zone, in the words of Cohen, she "worked like a fiend": five hours of sleep and one meal a day, at lunchtime, that consisted of soup and an orange. Why waste time eating when one could be working? Even in her nineties, Rita always appeared with her white hair beautifully coiffed, in a white lab coat accessorized with high heels, and wielding her instruments with manicured hands.

Like the Roman God Janus, Rita had two sides: one, the mathematical, the other, the dramatic. With her artistic flair, she illustrated many of her research papers with imaginative sketches and even designed her own jewelry. She was colorful when she spoke in heavily accented Italian, sometimes too much so for the plain language of science. When one neuroscientist toned down the description of their findings in a joint paper, she accused him of turning her beautiful prose into boiled spinach. He countered by calling her a cross between Marie Curie and Maria Callas. Rita also garnered a reputation for eccentricity; in the 1950s, she carried experimental mice in her handbag from St. Louis to Brazil. In Rio de Janeiro, she set up a research project in a state-of-the-art laboratory that had the facilities she required—a far cry from her youthful bedroom workstation.

An advantage of living to your seventh decade is that you tend to have the last word. Dr. Levi-Montalcini saw her theories rebuffed throughout the 1950s and 1960s, but she received validation in 1986, when she won the Nobel Prize for Medicine, an award only four women had received. Wearing an elegant black velvet gown, she accepted, along with Stanley Cohen, the honor for their research on NGF. Her reaction to the astonishing news was that the award was "a great honor but there is no great thrill as the moment of discovery." At one of the numerous celebrations, Rita claimed her brain was more vigorous than it had been four decades ago. She stated, "If I'm not mistaken, I can say my mental capacity is greater than when I was twenty because it has been enriched by so many experiences, in the same way that my curiosity and desire to be close to those who suffer has not diminished." Her country spared no expense to honor its Nobel recipient, the only Italian woman who had achieved the world's most prestigious prize in the field of science, showering her with receptions and further honors. The one she appreciated above all others was a decision by a university to gift to her research institute a generous grant of 448,000 pounds. Proving that she harbored no ill feelings toward her native land that had once driven her into hiding, she said, "I say to the young, be happy that you were born in Italy because of the beauty of the human capital, both masculine and feminine, of this country."

The elderly woman winning the Nobel Prize launched untold interest in the diminutive doctor's fascinating life, and consequently, the scientist turned author with her autobiography, *In Praise of Imperfection*. The title seemed a strange choice for the perfectionist, but Levi-Montalcini unraveled the mystery when she wrote, "It is imperfection—not perfection—that is the end result of the program written into that formidably complex engine that is the human brain, and of the influences exerted upon us by the environment and whoever takes care of us during the long years of our physical, psychological, and intellectual development." With her words, she praised her supportive family and beloved nanny.

As well as being an eminent scientist, Dr. Levi-Montalcini was active in cultural, political, and social affairs. She served as a goodwill ambassador for the United Nations; established, with her twin, the Levi-Montalcini Foundation, dedicated to their father, to assist young people in their career paths; and was the first female admitted to the Pontifical Academy of Sciences that advises the Vatican, a heady honor for a non-Catholic. In 2001, at age ninety-two, the Italian parliament made her a senator for life, a title bestowed only on the most revered. In that position, from 2005 to 2007, she played a vital role in supporting the center-left government.

Rita's Nobel Prize remains a testimony to her brilliance; however, a comment she made showed she was also a noble woman. On Dr. Levi-Montalcini's 100th birthday, she spoke in Rome at a ceremony in her honor. Rita, with her white hair elegantly coiffed, and wearing a tailored navy blue suit, raised a glass of sparkling wine in a toast to her longevity. Recalling the years Mussolini had forced her underground, she stated, "Above all, don't fear difficult moments. The best comes from them."

CHAPTER EIGHT

I Am Unworthy (1910)

In "Starry, Starry Night," Don McLean's paean to Vincent van Gogh, McLean sang of the doomed artist, "But I could've told you, Vincent/This world was never meant for one as beautiful as you." The lyrics could also describe a woman whose wrinkled visage and shrunken body placed a light in a darkened sky.

If ever a person embodied the biblical proverb that faith can move mountains, it was Gonxha (Rosebud) Agnes Bojaxhiu, from Skopje, in a Muslim area of present-day Yugoslavia. In addition to being a member of a religious minority, her father, Nikola, who fought for Albanian autonomy, died when she was eight: Rumor has it that his demise was at the hand of Serbian agents. A further hardship was her club foot and susceptibility to malaria and whooping cough. Dranafile, widowed mother of three, kept despair at bay through her staunch Roman Catholic faith.

While most preteens dream of clothes, parties, and boys, Gonxha knew there could only be one man in her life, Jesus, and she resolved to be a nun. At age eighteen, devastated at leaving her mother, Gonxha boarded a ship to the Order of Loreto in Ireland, a choice dictated by its sisters who worked in India, the country she knew was her destiny. She adopted the name Sister Mary Teresa of the Child Jesus—after St. Therese, "Little Flower," who, in 1897, at the age twenty-four, died of tuberculosis in a convent at Lisieux. Later that year, she journeyed to her promised land of Calcutta, where she taught geography at St. Mary's, an exclusive girls' school. The building was near the notorious Motijhil slum, and between classes, Sister Mary Teresa delivered medicine and clothing to the poor. She took her final vows in 1937, and as Mother

Teresa, became the headmistress. Although she was popular among her students, letters from her mother reinforced her own conviction that her fate lay beyond the walls of her sheltered enclave.

Mother Teresa's purpose appeared while the thirty-six-year-old was on a train bound for Darjeeling, when she received her "call within a call." She entertained no doubt that the message came from God ordering her to be His light: to serve the poorest of the poor and to live among them. To her great chagrin, there were obstacles in starting her own Order: no money, no accommodation, no backing from the Church in Rome. There was also the issue of getting released from her Loreto vows. Yet, with Mother Teresa's steely willpower, and her equally strong faith that God would admit no impediment, she soldiered on. In 1948, a year and a day after India became an independent nation, Mother Teresa left her upscale school for the streets and slums of Calcutta, armed with five rupees and immeasurable drive. To blend more easily with the downtrodden she had set herself to serve, she adopted the garb of the women who swept the streets as her new habit—a white cotton sari with three sky-blue stripes; her only adornment was a small cross. Upon completion of a nurses' training course with the Medical Missionaries at Patna, though inclined to faint at the sight of blood, she ventured into the pestilential horrors of Calcutta. Two years later, she won canonical recognition for her new order, the Missionaries of Charity. The sisters who joined her took vows of chastity, obedience, and service. Their adherence to poverty was extreme because, as their indefatigable leader explained, "To be able to love the poor and know the poor, we must be poor ourselves." Each member possessed two sets of clothes, wearing one while she washed the other in a bucket. When people suggested her Order should have fans, as the heat was intolerable, she replied, "The poor whom they are to serve have no fans. Most of the girls come from village homes where they had no fans. They should not be more comfortable here than at home." Under pain of expulsion, its members could not leave their living quarters without permission, entertain guests, or receive private mail. In addition, the strict rules forbade them to watch films, read novels, or call each other by nicknames. The sisters rescued newborn babies abandoned in garbage bins, sought out the sick, and took in lepers and the mentally ill. They taught the street children how to read by drawing letters in the dirt. The first woman the nun rescued lay dying in a gutter, half eaten by rats. "I knew she was dying," the diminutive dynamo said. "After I did what I could, she took my hand, gave me a beautiful smile and thanked me. She gave me more than I gave her."

Mother Teresa's mission was to alleviate the suffering of the Untouchables—the lowest caste of Indian society—but at that time she was an unknown Albanian nun nearing age forty, armed with nothing more than faith. As it transpired, faith proved enough, along with her single-minded devotion. She approached the local government and, under her relentless onslaught, they offered her a building that had fallen into disrepair, one local thugs used as a gambling den. Mother Teresa and her Order, which had increased to twenty-six, moved in. Then they went in search of the destitute and the dying. In the humble structure, the nuns provided clean sheets, clean clothing, and a clean environment for those at death's door. The Order christened the building Nirmal Hriday, the place for the pure of heart. Further undertakings continued: mobile health clinics, centers for the hungry, hospices for lepers and victims of AIDS, homes for alcoholics and drug addicts, shelters for the homeless. Mother Teresa gladly accepted donations to fund her enterprises. She liked to say that money was "really no problem, we depend on divine providence." And for the times when providence did not come through, she resorted to her own tactics. Once, having bought $800 worth of groceries for the needy, she refused to move from the checkout line until someone paid the bill. Similarly, as she flew around the world visiting the places she had once taught her geography class about, she resented the cost of the tickets, money that could have been earmarked for charity. She offered to work as a hostess in lieu of a ticket; the owners did not take her up on her offer, but the government agreed tickets on Indian airlines and railroads would be complimentary. Eventually, the Missionaries of Charity expanded to ninety countries and the woman with the shrunken body and cavernous eyes seemed to be everywhere at once. In 1982, at age seventy-two, she worked for a number of days in Beirut, Lebanon, crisscrossing the Green Line that divided Christian East Beirut from Muslim West Beirut. She rescued dozens of mentally ill children from the dangers of warfare in the Muslim sector of the city. In 1986, she escaped unscathed when her plane crashed in Tanzania.

After a visit, Pope Paul VI gifted Mother Teresa the white Lincoln Continental whose air-conditioning saved him from the sweltering Indian heat. She immediately raffled it off, earning many times more than would have been gained by an outright sale. When told she should keep the gift for her Order, she replied, "Just think of how many orphans I could feed." Although she was well known for years in religious circles, her international reputation really took off through Malcolm Muggeridge's 1969 BBC film, *Something Beautiful for God.* The movie evoked a huge buzz and made the nun into an international star. Before long, she was sharing television studios with David Frost, Norman Mailer, and Barbara Walters. The Saint of the Gutter, as the media dubbed her, dealt with the mighty in the same manner as she did the humble. Upon meeting Queen Elizabeth II, Mother Teresa casually asked about Her Majesty's latest grandchild; she gave Prime Minister Margaret Thatcher a plastic statuette of the Virgin Mary. She told the Prince of Wales, "You know you could not do my work and I could not do yours. We are both working for God."

News of the little woman who did great acts resulted in Mother Teresa's nomination for the Nobel Prize in 1979, when she was sixty-nine years old. The nun with her simple gold cross stood in marked contrast to the glittering jewels worn by the world's elite. Not surprisingly, she used the $190,000 award for the betterment of others. She explained, "Just think of how many orphans I can feed." When word first broke that she was to be a candidate for the Peace Prize, the international press descended on her mission in droves. Self-effacing when it came to personal glory, Mother Teresa told her sisters, "I am going to hide somewhere."

Yet, not everyone was in Camp Mother Teresa; uber-feminist Germaine Greer launched a full-blooded attack on the nun for her anti-abortion views. Christopher Hitchens' 1995 book, *The Missionary Position*, and his 1994 documentary, *Hell's Angel*, were highly critical of what he felt was a holier-than-thou woman; he described her as a "Catholic fundamentalist with a mission against abortion and some rather dodgy friends." The latter was in reference to the Haitian dictator Baby Doc Duvalier, whose ill-gotten gains were accepted into the Order's coffers. Other critics chimed in by claiming the Missionaries of Charity could better serve the world by providing condoms rather than charity. Mother Teresa's response, "Forgive them, for they know not what they do."

A life of traversing the world's most dangerous places in saris and sandals, sleeping four hours a night, and subsisting on a meager diet of dhal and rice never fazed the living saint. However, a low period in her life occurred when Dranafile was dying, and her sixty-two-year-old daughter could not be with her because of Albania's communist regime. Mother Teresa prayed nonstop and stormed the Albanian Embassy in Rome for help. Her considerable power of rhetoric convinced a group of prominent individuals, including Indira Gandhi, to intervene with the government. However, to Mother Teresa's dismay, Enver Hoxha's anti-religious administration ignored all her pleas. The fervently Catholic Dranafile's burial place could not bear a cross, per the regime. Her daughter, who had not seen her mother since she left home, accepted her sorrow as the will of God.

A half-century of tireless devotion gnarled her hands, creased her face, and bent her back (she was only four feet ten inches tall), and her late-in-life appearance became the photographic icon that held a mirror to the conscience of the world. At age eighty, she suffered a heart attack while visiting the Pope, and doctors implanted a pacemaker. Mother Teresa sent in her resignation as head of the Missionaries of Charity to Pope John Paul II, stating that she was stepping down from the Order she had launched. "The time," she said, had come for "younger hands." Nevertheless, when it came time to step down, she decided not to relinquish her role because she believed it was God's will she continue in the path He had chosen for her long ago. Death held no terror for the woman who had lived alongside it for most of her life. In a reverential tone, she expressed her faith saying, "Heaven for me will be the joy of being with Jesus and Mary and all of the other saints and angels, and all our poor, all going home to God." The woman, who had undergone the name changes from Gonxha Agnes Bolaxhiu, to Sister Mary Teresa, to Mother Teresa, became Saint Teresa with her 2016 canonization. No doubt she would have remarked upon the news of her beatification with the same words she had uttered when the Nobel Committee had called the nun with her nomination: "I am unworthy."

CHAPTER NINE

Chocolate (1912)

George Patton said, "Old generals never die. They just fade away." However, while riding off into the sunset may be the route for old generals, it is not necessarily the path for entertainers who are reluctant to take their final bow. Some '60s-era rockers continue to perform: Mick Jagger is still belting out rock hits, Willie Nelson is still strumming country, Ozzy Osbourne is still gyrating to heavy metal. But these musicians are mere babes in the woods compared to the Queen of Operetta whose silvery soprano made her a human nightingale.

In the Grimm Brothers' tale, the fairies gifted Sleeping Beauty with beauty, goodness, and grace, while an evil one condemned her to prick her finger on a spindle and die. The non-fictional counterpart to the Germanic Briar Rose was Marta Eggerth, born in Budapest to a banker father, who was also a talented amateur pianist, and an operatic soprano mother, who gave up her singing career to raise her daughter. A vocal prodigy, Marta's first love was opera, and she landed her first stage role by singing "Un bel di" from Puccini's *Madame Butterfly*; she was eleven at the time. The press declared her "Hungary's National Idol," and her stunning success led to a concert tour of Denmark, Holland, and Sweden. At age fourteen, a pivotal operatic experience for Marta was watching a production of *Turandot* that starred the Polish tenor Jan Kiepura, then twenty-four, a matinee idol who foreshadowed the Three Tenors. Marta later recalled that she felt he was her Prince Charming, and revealed, "I fell in love. I waited for him on the street. But there were so many girls, he didn't even notice me."

Eggerth performed classical arias until Emmerich Kálmán invited her to Vienna to perform in his operetta *The Violet of Montmartre*, as an understudy for Adele Kern. She became Europe's *wunderkind* when she took over for the star after she came down with a sore throat. The opportunity led to another role as the chambermaid in Max Reinhardt's Hamburg production of Johan Strauss II's *Die Fledermaus*. Although she played a vulgar domestic onstage, offstage she met famed musicians. In her teens, she performed at Berlin's Hungarian Embassy; as she had no pianist, "a little tiny old man sat down and played for me so divinely that I almost stopped singing." Afterwards, she told him that he played so beautifully he should be a professional pianist. His reply, "You think so? You don't think I'm too old for it?" The great Austrian-Jewish keyboard artist Artur Schnabel was pulling her leg. Another brush with a famed musician occurred when she was staying in a Vienna hotel and conductor Otto Klemperer requested the use of her piano. When she returned, the room was thick with cigar smoke, and there were, inexplicably, his socks on her bed.

The songbird's triumph proved a springboard in establishing the blonde-haired beauty as one of the brightest lights in German-language operetta, and Austro-Hungarian composer Franz Lehar composed music especially for the diva. Clemens Krauss offered to put her on salary at the Vienna State Opera if she agreed to stop singing in public for five years and spend all her time studying Mozart. Since five years seemed like an eternity to the seventeen-year-old, she declined. At this juncture, between the two world wars and during the silver age of Viennese operetta, Marta reigned supreme. Her blonde beauty and bell-like voice provided a welcome relief from ruinous inflation, worldwide depression, and the approaching sound of Nazi jackboots. Hitler loved Viennese operetta, dominated though it was by Jewish composers; the Führer's favorite was *Die Csardasfurstin (The Gypsy Princess)*, the film version of which included the half-Jewish Eggerth.

The German film directors came calling, and soon Marta was working in Berlin, where she made more than forty movies. In 1934, on the set of the aptly named *Mein Herz rufft nach Dir (My Heart is Calling You)*, Marta, after first seeing him on the screen eight years earlier, finally met her screen idol, Jan Kiepura. Initially, they disliked one another, but Marta found herself jealous when Jan filmed a romantic scene for the movie's French version and used mouth-spray before kissing actress Danielle Darrieux, something he did not do with her. Eventually, Jan took notice, and one evening escorted her to her door. Since she felt it too early in their relationship to ask him in, they walked up and down the street of the building where she lived. When they eventually came to say good-night, Kiepura hurried to a florist and bought Eggerth a huge bouquet of flowers. Since he did not have any money on him, Marta had to pay. Despite this unromantic start, they were married in 1936 and became known as *liebespaar*, the Love Pair.

Marta's spindle that threatened to silence her silver voice was the rise of Hitler; she and Jan were Nazi targets as their mothers were Jewish. Once the war broke out, Kiepura wanted to fight for his native Poland, but as the couple was in New York, where he was singing Rodolfo in Puccini's *La Boheme* at the Metropolitan Opera, he decided to concentrate his efforts on performing at fundraisers on behalf of his countrymen. Marta landed a studio contract with MGM, where she hobnobbed with other refugees; her mother used to play cards with fellow Hungarians Bela Lugosi and Peter Lorre. She made two films, *For Me and My Gal* (1942) and *Presenting Lily Mars* (1943) with Judy Garland. At an advance screening for the former movie, her big musical number was met with thunderous applause, but the next day, studio executives cut her scene. MGM was grooming Garland as its star, and Eggerth's rendition of *The Spell of the Waltz* was edging in on Judy's glory. Marta was miserable; she hated being on the opposite coast from her husband, and as someone who had always had the lead roles, she bitterly resented playing second

fiddle. After endless pleading with Louis B. Mayer, in 1943,
he released her from her contract, and she and her husband
performed Lehar's *The Merry Widow* operetta on Broadway,
choreographed by George Balanchine. Marta was the greatest
of Widows, and their dual role brought glamour to wartime
New York. They performed the act two thousand times in
five languages (Marta spoke six, though five were accented
with her native Hungarian). The play provided them with
money to set up a comfortable life and replace the extensive
possessions they had lost in their European exodus. Kiepura
had invested most of his money ($3 million) in Poland, where
he had built a grand hotel, Patria, that is still operating today.
During the war, the Polish government confiscated it, and the
couple spent years trying to reclaim their stolen property.

   The Kiepuras returned to Europe after the war, taking
The Merry Widow on the road and making several other films.
However, as their American citizenship application would
have expired had they stayed away more than five years, they
returned to the States, with sons Jan Jr. and Marjan in tow.
Marta and Jan bought their once-upon-a-time home in Rye,
north of New York City, and they decorated it with family
photographs and musical memorabilia. The home included
a piano that Vladimir Horowitz, the virtuoso, after trying out
a song, pronounced "not bad"; another esteemed guest was
Marion Anderson. On the piano's surface was a photograph of
an elderly Lehar who had once declared Marta "enchanting."

   Jan's sudden death from a heart attack in 1966 devastated
Ms. Eggerth, who became anything but a merry widow. The
composer Frederic Chopin had instructed that his body
be interred in the Cimetière du Père Lachaise in Paris, and
his heart laid to rest in the Holy Cross Chapel in his native
Poland; in the same vein, Kiepura requested that his remains
return to Warsaw. Having lost the love of her life, Marta vowed
she would never sing again. Eggerth held fast to this promise,
even when offered the coveted role in the original production
of *Cabaret.* But Marta could no more stop singing than one

could stop breathing, and with the encouragement of her mother, the steadfast fixture in her life, Eggerth applied the greasepaint once more. After a lifetime of frenetic activity, the thought of idleness was anathema, and to keep busy, she gave master classes on Viennese operetta at the Manhattan School of Music. At age seventy-two, she worked opposite Diana Rigg in the musical *Colette* and starred in Stephen Sondheim's *Follies*. In 1999, seventy years after her debut, Marta returned to the Vienna State Opera, where she reprised a medley from *The Merry Widow* in four languages. News of the famed daughter's homecoming produced a rush for tickets, and her performance kept the audience spellbound. This return to the stage was a considerable feat for an eighty-seven-year-old. Afterwards, an elderly passerby stopped her in the street and inquired, "Excuse me," he asked, "weren't you once Marta Eggerth?" She was still every iota Marta Eggerth.

The operetta star, likened to opera great Maria Callas, received an invitation in 2005 to engage in a cabaret evening at the Sabarsky, a Viennese-style café in New York City's Neue Galerie museum. Apprehensive about booking a ninety-three-year-old, they asked her son if she would be able to perform for forty-five minutes. Marjan, a pianist who had looked after his mother's career and worked with her on the release of her CD set covering seven decades of entertainment, produced on his own label, said she was up to the task. As it turned out, Marta, dressed in a sparkly gown, gave them an hour and a half. Interacting with the audience, Eggerth said, "My life is an open book. I'll let you know everything, even my age." Marta commented on her long life, saying, "I'm an old bag who doesn't feel her age. As long as I can do something and stay active I'm happy." Her career had always kept her so busy that she did not have time to bask in her success. In 1932, when she had acted in *The Blue from the Sky,* she never got to see it; her mother had merely pronounced it "good." She finally viewed it for the first time in 2010, when the Museum of Modern Art in New York included it as part of the *Weimar Cinema: 1913-1933* season. The announcement of her presence drew gasps of amazement from the audience. She was still able to hum along to the music. Throughout her nineties, Marta continued to sing, always in perfect pitch, and her repertoire usually included her signature rendition, *Wien, Nur Du Allenin (Vienna, City of My Dreams)*.

At age ninety-three, sitting in an armchair in her elegant home, she opened up about her out-of-the-ordinary life. She said, "I never want to be one of those singers with a wobble. If I develop a wobble, I will quit immediately." Marjan's rejoinder was, "We'll fire you, Mom." Her career remained secure. She attributed the longevity of her voice to the fact that she never stayed out late, drank, or smoked, and declared she had always been a "prisoner of my voice." After she declared herself a teetotaler, the interviewer asked her about her well-known love of tokay, the Hungarian wine. Her tongue-in-cheek response: "Tokay, this is medicine!" chortled Marta with a pitying smile for one who could be so ignorant. How can one argue with a ninety-something diva? Eggerth concluded, "I have had ten lives. But if I want to realize all my plans, I'll have to live until I'm three hundred." She did not quite reach that age, as she passed away at 101 in her home; it was time to rejoin her *liebespaar*. At age ninety-nine, Marta had given her last public performance in 2011. In a fitting testament to the sweetness of her life, she had asked to be paid in chocolate.

CHAPTER TEN

If Those Hats Could Talk (1912)

Forrest Gump, sitting on a park bench, has a one-sided conversation with a disinterested nurse and tells her, "Momma always says there's an awful lot you could tell about a person by their shoes. Where they're going. Where they've been. I've worn lots of shoes." Forrest obsessed over his footwear in much the same way as a fellow Southerner was concerned with her hats, and during her nine decades, both literally and figuratively, she wore any number of them.

The lady who devoted almost a century of her life as a foot soldier for equality was born in a time and place where justice was in short supply. In the belief there would be less racism in the North than in the former capital of the Confederacy, James Height and his wife, Fannie, migrated to the North. The family that included Dorothy, Anthanette, Josephine, and Jessie ended up in Rankin, near Pittsburg. Dorothy was self-conscious about her five-foot-nine-inch height that she reached at age eleven, and her severe asthma led to the prognosis that she would not survive her teens. In addition to her medical troubles, she had to confront Jim Crow, the first gentleman of racism. Dorothy's first lash of racial bigotry occurred when she was eight years old, and her best friend Sally Hay explained she could no longer play with her because she was a "nigger." Childhood griefs linger, and at age twelve, Dorothy was denied entrance to a YWCA pool; when she demanded an explanation, the director informed her girls of color were not welcome. A rival basketball team cancelled a competition because Dorothy was not Caucasian. On one occasion, racism came with a silver lining. In 1928, a new principal arrived at the nearly all-white Rankin High, and his directive forbade Dorothy, who usually led the singing at school assemblies, from doing so again. At the first assembly after his order, when the pianist began the alma mater, the students stayed silent. The accompanist tried twice more, with the same result. Finally, the principal motioned Dorothy to the stage, and this time a chorus of youthful voices filled the air. The fact that Dorothy could inspire such solidarity among her white peers in pre-Depression America presaged the greatness that was to follow.

During Height's senior year, she entered an Elks-sponsored national speech contest on the Constitution, and she was the only non-white in the auditorium except for the janitor. Her topic was the Fourteenth Amendment, intended to extend Constitutional protections to former slaves and their descendants. The jury awarded her first prize: a four-year college scholarship. Barnard College accepted her application, but shortly before classes began, the Dean realized the college already admitted its quota of black students: two. Clutching her Barnard acceptance letter, Dorothy took the subway to New York University who accepted her on the spot. She received a bachelor's in education and a master's in psychology. To earn money, Dorothy took odd jobs, such as ironing entertainer Eddie Cantor's shirts and proofreading Marcus Garvey's newspaper, *The Negro World*. She went nightclubbing in Harlem, where she met poet Langston Hughes. Height also became heavily involved in the Civil Rights Movement; whenever there was a lynching in the South, she demonstrated in Times Square, heart and black armband on her sleeve. Height often quoted the nineteenth-century abolitionist Frederick Douglass, who said the three effective ways to fight for justice were "agitate, agitate, agitate."

Upon graduation, Height worked as a social worker for the New York City welfare department. However, after attending an international youth conference in Oxford in 1937, Dorothy felt she needed to make more of an impact, and left for a position at the Harlem YWCA. One month later, she met Mary McLeod Bethune and Eleanor Roosevelt on the same day.

Mrs. Bethune, the daughter of slaves, was hosting a meeting of the National Council of Negro Women, and the First Lady was to be the guest speaker. The twenty-five-year-old Ms. Height had the role of escort for the esteemed guest, but this singular opportunity almost did not happen when Mrs. Roosevelt entered through the service entrance and was making her way on her own. Seeing her honor going up in smoke, Dorothy later recounted, "Who would have thought that Mrs. Roosevelt would park her own car on a Harlem street and come through the service entrance?" Fortunately, Dorothy was able to intercept her. The First Lady gave a rousing speech, and at its close, the ladies serenaded her with "Let Me Call You Sweetheart." After Eleanor's departure, Mary made her fingers into a fist to impress upon her followers the importance of women working together to eliminate injustice in the dual spheres of racism and sexism. She told her protégées, "The freedom gates are half-ajar. We must pry them fully open." Dorothy picked up the baton, and Mary's words became the title of Height's memoir, *Wide the Freedom Gates*, published at age ninety-one. The author dedicated it to "my loving mother, Fannie Burroughs Height, and her great expectations."

The girl who had not been able to dip her toes in the pool of the Rankin Y eventually became the director of its office for racial justice. Her first act was to call attention to the exploitation of black domestic day laborers. The women, who congregated on street corners in Brooklyn and the Bronx, known locally as slave markets, were picked up and hired for fifteen cents an hour by white suburban housewives who cruised the corners in their cars. On Height's agenda was the push to end the organization's practice of separate conferences, one for white leaders and one for blacks. Heads of local chapters in the South refused to meet with her, and she spent nights with local African-American families because hotels would not admit black guests. A white police officer threatened her life when she defied his order to wait for a train in the "colored waiting room" rather than on the platform with her white colleagues. In response, her friends surrounded her, and together they entered the train. When one of the leaders of the NAACP heard of the incident, he said, "Dorothy, had you been a black man, you would have been dead." Through her position, she collaborated with the civil rights movement's key figures, referred to as the Big Six. Height made seven, but they discounted her contributions because she was female.

Throughout her thirty years at the YWCA, Dorothy spent most of her free time volunteering for the National Council of Negro Women, something she did for the next forty years. She created "Wednesdays in Mississippi," a 1960s program that brought together Southern and Northern blacks and whites. She organized voter registration drives and set up day-care facilities, school breakfast programs, and job fairs. Ms. Height also initiated "pig banks" that provided livestock for poor families. Another accomplishment was the Black Family Reunion Celebration, a three-day cultural event in Washington, DC, with related events throughout the country, to help mend African-Americans' fractured families, where the babies' fathers were often AWOL. Height's mission was to help her sisterhood combat what she called the "triple bind of racism, sexism, and poverty." She stepped down as its president at age eighty-five but still made daily visits, using a walker or a wheelchair, as she became infirm. The council celebrated her birthday every year with an "Uncommon Height" gala fundraiser. On her ninetieth birthday, well-wishers such as Oprah Winfrey raised $5 million to pay off the organization's mortgage on its national headquarters at 633 Pennsylvania Avenue in Washington, the site of what was once a slave market.

Height's activism led to her sitting at arm's length from Dr. King as he delivered his "I Have a Dream" speech during the 1963 March on Washington. The photographers airbrushed Dorothy, sporting a patterned hat, out of the iconic photograph and the historic moment. She had appealed to Bayard Rustin, the event's chief organizer, to allow her to speak, to give women a voice, but the plea proved futile. The only female heard that day was Mahalia Jackson, the gospel vocalist. Ironically, had it not been for Height, there would have been no immortal address. Due to time constraints, each speaker had an allotment of seven minutes; Dorothy made the case that King should be the last at the podium, so his oration could go over time. In 1995, Ms. Height was among the few women to speak at the Million Man March on the Mall, led by Louis Farrakhan, chief minister of the Nation of Islam. Two years later, at eighty-five, she sat on the podium all day, in the whipping wind and rain, at the Million Woman March in Philadelphia. Less than a month later, at King's request, Dorothy was in Birmingham, Alabama to minister to the families of the four little black girls who had perished in a church bombing. In 1968, Height rushed to the White House, where she and her colleagues tried to advise President Lyndon B. Johnson on how to minimize black protests and rioting in the wake of Dr. King's assassination. Ms. Height was the warrior woman amongst men; her quest was to make her people realize that racial prejudice and gender prejudice were on the same side of the contaminated coin. With Gloria Steinem, Shirley Chisholm, and Betty Friedman, Dorothy helped found the National Women's Political Caucus in 1971.

Dorothy, who had embarked on social activism in her teens, never lost her momentum. Her retirement from her position at the YMCA ended at age sixty-three, but she only did it so that she could don another hat. She became a visiting professor at the Delhi School of Social Work in India. One of her oft-repeated sayings was, "If the times aren't ripe, you have to ripen the times," and she forever practiced what she preached.

As was the case with Forrest Gump, Height was present at many of America's pivotal moments: When President John F. Kennedy signed the Equal Pay Act, Ms. Height was at the White House to witness the ceremony. In recognition of her seven decades of advocacy for racial equality, the grande dame of the Civil Rights Movement, who always wore her signature hats, received a host of accolades. President Ronald Reagan presented her with the Presidential Citizens Medal, President Bill Clinton awarded her the Presidential Medal of Freedom, and President Bush gave her the Congressional Medal of Honor. Other tributes were her inclusion in the National Women's Hall of Fame and a spot on the podium at Barack Obama's inauguration. On the academic front, Ms. Height received three dozen honorary doctorates from institutions including Tuskegee, Harvard, and Princeton. But there was one academic award, the equivalent of a bachelor's degree, that resonated: In 2004, seventy-five years after turning her away, Barnard College designated Dorothy an honorary graduate.

In a nod to poetic justice, the woman who left her stamp on history received a postage stamp bearing her image in a wide-brimmed purple hat. The unveiling took place at the Rankin Christian Center, the site of her youthful affront. Dorothy passed away at age ninety-eight, fighting 'til the end to make the Fourteenth Amendment a right nationally acknowledged. Her spirit lives on in a collection of her 250 hats: the white mink she wore to present First Lady Mrs. Roosevelt the Mary Bethune Humanitarian Award, the rhinestone-encrusted one she wore at a gala of the Delta Sigma Theta Sorority, and the red, white, and blue one she sported at the Democratic Convention that nominated Barack Obama. If those hats could talk, what a tale they would tell.

CHAPTER ELEVEN

The Bumblebee (1916 or 1918)

Pink is the signature color for a number of icons: the plastic princess Barbie, the too-cute feline of Hello Kitty fame, the teenaged ladies from *Grease*. Yet, one lady predated these bright-hued females, and her relationship with pink left her rolling in the green.

"You can do it, Mary Kay!" These were the words of encouragement Lulu Wagner gave her youngest child, Mary Kathlyn Wagner. With Lulu's husband bedridden from a bout of tuberculosis and her 5:00 a.m. to 9:00 p.m. daily shift as a waitress in the whistle-stop town of Hot Wells, Texas, she had precious little else to offer. As Mary Kay's siblings had left home, the seven-year-old was left with the care of her father and the household chores. An overachiever, all through school she out-typed, out-debated, and outshone her classmates. When her best friend could afford to go to college and Mary Kay could not, she managed to upstage her friend at age seventeen when she married musician Ben Rogers, a member of a local band, the Hawaiian Strummers. Unable to afford a place of their own, the couple occupied a bedroom at her mother's house. Upon Ben's return from duty in World War II, he demanded a divorce; it was not only his guitar he strummed. Although Mary Kay acknowledged their marriage had cracks, the desertion left her at the lowest point of her life. However, with three children to raise—deadbeat dad was MIA—rather than wallow in depression, she peddled housewares for Stanley Home Products, a direct sales company. After three weeks, she borrowed twelve dollars to travel to the company's annual convention in Dallas, where that year's Queen of Sales won an alligator bag as a reward. For the next year, she carried a picture of an alligator bag, and each week, she wrote her sales goals in soap on her bathroom mirror. At the next convention, the company crowned Mary Kay Queen; to her disappointment, her prize was a trophy.

In addition to despair at the demise of her marriage, Mary Kay was embittered by her employer, who denied her an opportunity to ascend the corporate ladder because she wore a skirt in a suit-and-tie world. The final straw for her was when the man she had trained received a position that made him her superior, earning twice her salary. In 1952, after twenty-five years of service, she quit. Mary Kay, in trademark Texas drawl, groused, "Those men didn't believe a woman had brain matter at all. I learned back then that as long as men didn't believe women could do anything, women were never going to have a chance."

Mary Kay's next foray into business was at World Gift Co., a home accessories firm. During her eleven-year employment, through her indefatigable efforts, distribution expanded into forty-three states. Stricken in 1957 by a disease characterized by uncontrollable spasms that twisted the left side of her face into a permanent grimace, despite preoccupation about her looks, she wore sunglasses until she could afford medical treatment. The term "glass ceiling" had yet to be coined; however, Mary Kay bumped her perfectly coiffed head on it time after time until she resigned in 1963.

At age forty-five, Mrs. Hallenback—the surname of her second husband George—was unwilling to admit defeat, but was understandably reluctant to attempt a third foray into the patriarchy who responded to her suggestions with, "Oh, Mary Kay, you're thinking just like a woman." On a memorable morning—one that was to change her life and those of untold women—Mary Kay sat at her kitchen table and made two lists on a yellow legal pad. On the first were the good experiences she had had in the business world and on the second were the bad experiences, such as the rampant sexism that allowed only males to sit at the top of the hierarchy and command the big bucks. After staring at the paper, the middle-aged matron slapped her hand to her assisted blonde hair. She realized she could turn her lists into a blueprint for a dream company—staffed with a female workforce who had to juggle the demands of career and child care. Her vision entailed the idea that, instead of trying to crack the old boys' network, ladies could strike out on their own. Now that she had a plan, she had to come up with a product.

Mary Kay derived the idea for a skin-care line from Ova Heath Spoonemore, a hostess at a Stanley Home Products party where Mary Kay had been in attendance. When the official business ended, Ova had handed out jars with penciled labels to her guests, explaining they contained the secret to skin care. Her father, an Arkansas tanner, had given her the formula after he noticed his hands looked younger than his face due to the solutions. Mary Kay had been using it for a decade and said that after a Stanley demonstration, clients would invariably ask, "We know about that bowl cleaner. Tell us what you did to your face." Mary Kay bought the rights to the product for $500, found a way to get rid of its skunk-scent odor, and packaged it in pink. George, who had planned to go into business with his wife, had died a month earlier from a heart attack at their kitchen table. She decided to carry on with her plan that entailed investing her savings of $5,000, despite the advice of her lawyer and accountant, who tried to dissuade her from striking out on her own. She offered this explanation of her refusal to back down: "The answer is I was middle-aged, had varicose veins and I didn't have time to fool around. Have you heard the definition of a woman's needs? From fourteen to forty, she needs good looks, from forty to sixty, she needs personality, and I'm here to tell you that after sixty, she needs cash."

The eponymous business opened with nine saleswomen and Mary Kay's twenty-year-old son, Richard Rogers. Its philosophy embraced the founder's mantra: God first, family second, career third. Another guiding light was that being female was not a liability. Beauty by Mary Kay, its initial name,

debuted in a five-hundred-square-foot storefront manned by
nine of her closest gal pals. All products were pink and sold by
consultants on a private basis. In an era when women could
not sign their names on bank loans, Mary Kay cosmetics
offered the housewife financial opportunities as well as self-
esteem.

By the mid 1980s, the company was at its zenith,
and some twenty thousand preening beauty consultants
swooped into the Dallas Convention Center in full plumage:
arched brows penciled in, a flurry of false eyelashes, and
rouged cheeks. En masse, their flawlessly polished, razor-
sharp fingernails could have readily put a sizeable dent
in an armored car. But the ladies were not bent on acts of
destruction; rather, they had gathered to hear, cheer, and
revere their founder. Mary Kay Ash, the mascaraed Moses, led
these women to the promised land of financial autonomy.
She often quoted from a book entitled *Rhinoceros Success*:
"Don't sit back and be a cow, be a six-thousand-pound rhino.
Charge!" The diminutive leader micromanaged every aspect
of her empire, even on the cusp of age seventy. She was
always coy as to the year of her birth and commented, "A
woman who will tell her age will tell anything."

In a brilliant stroke of marketing, Mary Kay organized
annual seminars where her top-grossing consultants were
publicly feted. The initial 1964 get-together took place in a
warehouse decorated with balloons and crepe paper, and the
high priestess of pink cooked chicken for two hundred people
and made the jalapeno dressing and Jell-O salad, served
on paper plates. The prizes became ever glitzier: diamond
baubles, coats that once were on the backs of minks, and the
crème de la crème, a pink Cadillac. (Winners received a pink
Mercedes in Germany and a pink Toyota in Taiwan.) By 1994,
consultants had claimed seven thousand cars, valued at more
than $100 million. The prizes were presented amidst a show
that rivaled those in Las Vegas. At the close of the evening,
the emcee would introduce the head honcho, known as the

Queen of Queens, who would waltz to the microphone to conclude the evening, saying, "God didn't have time to make a nobody, only a somebody!"

Mary Kay's wealth allowed her to dress in sequined splendor, a mink stole draped over her shoulders, an alligator bag on her arm, but the girl from hole-in-the-wall Hot Wells never lost touch with her roots. In her elaborate galas, often attended by representatives from the Harvard School of Business, she would startle a maid sneaking a smoke by a dumpster and address her as if she were the earth's only other inhabitant, "How are you?" Then, leaving the woman behind in her well-perfumed wake, "You're great! Fake it till you make it!"

Mary Kay's indefatigable spirit never deserted, even when she found herself single for the third time upon the death of Mel Ash, the husband who had provided the happiest of her marriages. The widow explained her refusal to take a fourth foray into matrimony by saying that the available pool of men were seeking someone who would provide a purse and a nurse. She explained, "There are a lot of affluent men at my church (Baptist) who are dateable, but they're scared to death of me because they consider me so much more successful— and that's threatening to a man's ego." The diminutive rhinoceros charged ahead until age seventy-eight, when a stroke obliged her to relinquish the reins of her company to her son.

Mary Kay turned down an avalanche of invitations, as she was disinterested in being a fixture in Dallas society. She explained, "I enjoy the Fortune 500 people but not as a steady diet. I'm not interested in yaw-ting or social functions." The fact that Mrs. Ash would rather have been at home was not surprising. Her $5 million mansion was a thirty-room pink palace, replete with Grecian pool, crystal chandeliers, and eleven bathrooms, one modeled after Liberace's, a dear friend. Acres of sea-green carpet flowed beneath the twenty-eight-foot-ceilings, and in the drawing-room stood a nine-foot grand piano that played a constant stream of Liberace cassettes. Of course, the garage housed a pink Cadillac. A security guard generally shadowed the diminutive multimillionaire, even as she pushed her cart at the local supermarket. In the evenings, the woman who owned 1.7 million shares of her company's stock was a devoted coupon clipper, intent on finding the best place to chow down on a chili dog. An ordinary evening *chez* Mrs. Ash was spent watching Hawaii Five-O reruns, poring over a condensed whodunit in a *Reader's Digest* collection, and sifting through the paperwork in her alligator bag. Before retiring, and after slathering Mary Kay creams on her face and body, she always made a list of six goals for the following day. One of these was to become an author, and she wrote the third of her autobiographies just shy of age eighty, *Mary Kay—You Can Have It All*. Her morning ritual entailed putting on a full face of makeup, including eyelashes, while in the background played motivational tapes. Mrs. Ash never left home without her diamond-studded bumble brooch, the size of a kumquat. It became the company symbol after Mary Kay learned that, aerodynamically, the bumblebee should not be able to fly—its wings are too fragile to hold up its plump body. Mary Kay commented, "It's just like our women who didn't know they could fly to the top, but they did."

CHAPTER TWELVE

Namaste (1918)

The word yogi conjures different images: an Indian practitioner of an ancient art; a famous Yankee catcher; a resident of Jellystone Park. Yogi is also associated with a woman whose life proves that, despite advanced age, one can still dance with the stars.

The latest breed of star to emerge from social media is the "yogalebrity"—young, lithe, Lycra-clad—who appears in body-contorting poses. But there is one who is an exception to this trend: a 100-year-old who, unlike the majority of these water-bottle-toting, sheathed-in-athletic-wear yogis, is a centenarian who rocks big earrings, brightly colored nails, and sky-high heels (except when doing yoga), and whose beverage of choice comes in red and white.

Tao Andree Porchon was born two months prematurely on a ship in the middle of the English Channel. Her mother, who was from India, died giving birth. Her French father entrusted Tao to his brother and moved to Canada to start a horse ranch. Tao grew up in Pondicherry, India, bilingual in French and Hindi, where her uncle, a follower of Hindu monk Swami Vivekananda, raised her on a vegetarian diet and the principles of his guru. She recalled that he "instilled in me a sense of freedom and curiosity to explore the energy in all things and in myself." His engineering job entailed building railroad systems throughout Asia and Africa, and his niece accompanied him, meeting Maasai tribesmen and Singapore merchants.

While her uncle encouraged her, others tried to extinguish her flame. At age eight, Tao was at the beach and spotted a group of boys contorting their bodies. She thought they were playing a game and wanted to join in the fun. Her aunt replied that they were practicing yoga, and such movements were "unladylike." Tao's rejoinder was if the boys could do it, she could do it as well. Another memorable occurrence took place when Tao was twelve; she came home and saw a little man sitting on the floor, and to her surprise, everyone was bowing to him. The stranger was Mohandas Gandhi, and a few months later, she and her uncle joined the Mahatma on his Salt March to the Sea, undertaken to wrest India from the yoke of the British Empire.

During the World War II years, Tao left for France after her uncle came under the Nazi radar for hiding British and French expatriates. There she met another aunt who initiated her into the world of wine and the Resistance. Tao helped her relative hide Jews in the cement wine vats at the Porchon vineyard in the Rhone Valley. On one of these missions, the Germans captured her partner, Joel Le Tac, who ended up in a concentration camp. Fearing she was next, Tao fled to England, where she continued the fight by working with General Charles de Gaulle. Despite the bombing of London, she worked in a nightclub, performing Indian dances for American troops, and befriending Marlene Dietrich and Noel Coward. Her seventeen-inch waist and impressive gams, described by the press as "the longest legs in Europe," were attributes that helped her obtain work as a model for Chanel.

In 1948, Porchon toured the United States, signed a contract with MGM, and hobnobbed with Hollywood honchos such as Cesar Romero, Burgess Meredith, Marilyn Monroe, and Fred Astaire. When Debbie Reynolds and Shirley MacLaine asked her to teach them yoga, she realized she had found her calling and returned to India where she resided for seventeen years to master the ancient art. The man known as the godfather of modern fitness, Jack LaLanne, gave Porchon her first paying job as an instructor.

In 1963, while travelling in New York, Tao's friend introduced her to insurance agent Bill Lynch. Although they had led very different lives, a commonality was their love of vino, and in 1967, they founded the American Wine Society. (Tao drinks only two beverages, tea and wine.) The couple settled in Hartsdale, New York, and, being childless, they focused on civic commitment. Bill died in 1982 in a motorcycle accident, and his grieving widow, left without relatives, threw herself into her career and founded the Westchester Institute of Yoga. At age 100, she gives classes up to twenty hours a week and has trained over three hundred instructors. Unfortunately, after three hip-replacement surgeries, she can no longer demonstrate all the poses. Due to her injuries, her doctor explained that her yoga days were a thing of the past. Undaunted, she completed physical therapy, and afterward mailed her physician a photo of herself in a raised lotus pose. She explained, "What you put in your mind materializes. I don't believe in fear and don't allow my mind to dwell on the negative."

News of the elderly yogi renowned for her suppleness and stamina spread, and workout guru Jane Fonda became an admirer. In class, Tao cuts a glamorous figure, and between adjusting a student's back or fine-tuning a hand position, she weaves tales from her colorful life, such as the time she was in attendance at Dr. King's historic address. One afternoon, at her studio, she recalled that when she had first arrived in London, her English was poor, and Noel Coward, in a Henry Higgins vein, taught her to repeat, "I presume that your presumptions are precisely incorrect, your sarcastic insinuations too obnoxious to be appreciated." The encounter between the playwright and Ms. Porchon-Lynch had taken place forty years earlier. When class ends, Tao hurries from the studio—her appointment book is always full—a colorful vision in bright stretch pants, slinky top, and peep-toe high heels, and takes off in her gray Smart Car. When she is not teaching, she pursues her other passion, competitive ballroom dancing. In one event, her Tango partner was a twenty-two-year-old, and her Cha Cha partner was twenty-nine. Teresa Kay-Aba Kennedy, a co-author of a biography of Porchon-Lynch, *Dancing Light: The Spiritual Side of Being Through the Eyes of a Modern Yoga Master,* remarked that, although she is fifty years younger than her friend, Tao's schedule exhausts her. The two women had travelled to California where the grande dame of yoga had headlined an event for Athleta, an athletic-wear company owned by Gap, at its store at the Grove in Los Angeles, where she also did a photo shoot. As a very rare elderly star on the yogalebrity circuit, she carries exceptional marketing potential. Athleta also featured Porchon-Lynch in its catalog for its "Power of She" campaign. Nancy Green, the company's president, stated, "Tao aligns perfectly with our mission. We are working hard to break stereotypes of what youth and wellness mean."

Tao's students have become her surrogate family, and her career took off because of them. Joyce Pines, a retired schoolteacher, applied to the Guinness World Records, and in 2012, Mrs. Porchon-Lynch became "The Oldest Living Yoga Teacher." Another pupil hired photographer Robert Sturman, whose work focuses on yogis, including unexpected practitioners such as prison inmates and wounded veterans, to do a photo shoot of Tao in Central Park. True to form, she showed up in a red flamenco dress and high heels. When Sturman questioned her choice to wear stilettoes in a park, she told him that is the only kind of shoe she wears, because they "help elevate her consciousness" and because she has a very pronounced arch. As a perk of his profession, Mr. Sturman, in Sir Walter Raleigh fashion, got to carry her through the muddy grass. He posted images of the occasion on his Facebook account that went viral. Kelly Kamm, a yoga instructor, shared her opinion as to the reason behind Ms. Porchon-Lynch's celebrity status: "It's like being a rock star; it's a one in a hundred-thousand chance. I think that people were so hungry for someone to look up to who wasn't a young, skinny, blond yogi in a bra top. Then came Tao." With her social media cred firmly established, Mrs. Porchon-Lynch is fielding invitations to yoga festivals from Bosnia to Dubai. She gave a class to fifteen thousand people in Times Square and released a DVD. Joann Burnham, a founder of the annual Nantucket Yoga Festival, states, "At this point, you can't have a yoga festival and not invite Tao. Being in her presence and seeing the expectations of what someone would think about someone her age and seeing all those expectations squashed is so incredible." Tao also works with the United Nations to bring more yoga into the world, and in 2011, she attended a world peace summit.

Tao is no stranger to the small screen. In 2015, Porchon-Lynch performed the samba and salsa to a standing ovation on *America's Got Talent*. Her partner, Vard Margaryn, was seventy years her junior, and the YouTube video garnered nearly one million views. Howard Stern, a judge on the show, called the performance "too mind-blowing for words." Tao recalled of the event, "My partner was seventy years younger than me, and he was throwing me around his neck!" A subsequent dance partner is even younger: Anton Bilozorov said, "I teach her about dance and she teaches me about life." Two years later, Carl Reiner showcased her on his HBO documentary *If You're Not in the Obit, Eat Breakfast*, which showed that depression does not have to walk hand in hand with those born before the Great Depression. Some guests were crooner Tony Bennett, actress Betty White, and yoga enthusiast Tao Porchon-Lynch. A non-fictional Peter Pan, Tao stated that, in her heart, she is forever in her twenties and has no intention of ever growing up.

In contrast to the show that celebrates the positive, Tao has encountered those who are ready to throw in the proverbial towel. She recalled an experience where a room full of seniors viewed the prospect of attempting yoga with a defeatist attitude. They were all sitting around, hunched over with despair, when she pranced in, wearing high heels, and asked if they were going to join her. Their response? "What? At our age!?" They were her juniors by many years. Porchon-

Lynch's philosophy, "You haven't seen enough of this earth and there is a lot more to see that is beautiful."

Embraced by big names in the spirituality world, Tao met Deepak Chopra in 2011 when he took part in a panel discussion with the Dalai Lama. Tao, who had been sitting in the audience, and is not of the shrinking-violet ilk, introduced herself. Dr. Chopra said, "All these gurus from India who have come and gone—Pattabhi Jois, Iyengar—she has met them all. It's incredible. Even His Holiness was totally impressed by her." Chopra hosted her for a Facebook chat, and within a day, the video had received 115,000 views and 1,500 shares.

Tao sums up her secret to her longevity as adhering to a diet where she never eats anything that once lived, and grabbing life with octopus hands. She says, "When you believe in something go and do it. Don't spend your time on useless thoughts and say, 'I'll do it tomorrow.' Tomorrow never comes." Ms. Porchon-Lynch, a poster child for being a kick-ass senior, proves that age does not mean taking a back seat to life. In recognition of her unstoppable spirit, let's make a toast—-compliments of The American Wine Society—to the yogi who interacted with more icons than Forrest Gump and gets men to carry her over rough patches: *Namaste*.

CHAPTER THIRTEEN

In Dixie (1923)

Visitors heed the siren call of New Orleans for different reasons: music lovers to visit the birthplace of jazz; fans of Tennessee Williams' *A Streetcar Named Desire* to experience its ambience; party-lovers to partake of Mardi Gras. Foodies make New Orleans their port of call because of a restaurant presided over by the Queen of Creole cuisine, though, rather than a tiara, a pink baseball cap crowns her snowy locks.

The establishment that is equal parts museum, art gallery, and café is owned by a celebrity chef not schooled in Paris's Cordon Bleu, but through the recipes that made up the meals of her childhood. Leah Lange, the eldest of eleven children—nine girls—was born in Madisonville, Louisiana, a small, segregated farming community nestled between the Tchefuncte River and Lake Pontchartrain. The sisters took turns with the cooking and subsisted on fish from the bayou, barnyard chickens, and pork from their pigs to complement garden vegetables. Her father, Charles, bore the burden of raising his large family on a Depression-era salary of fifty cents an hour. Leah later recalled of the lean years, "Father told us to pray for work every day. We'd go fishing in the mornings, so we could have perch and grits for breakfast—but a lot of times, man, it was just grits." Her mother, Hortense, was innovative, and when her daughters needed clothes, she transformed printed flour sacks into dresses. She also instilled in her offspring the ability to dream. After a storm, she would take them outside to look at the rainbow, to illustrate that good followed bad.

Since Madisonville had no high school for black students, Leah Lange took the road less travelled and moved to New Orleans, where she boarded with her aunt and attended the all-girl, all-black, Catholic St. Mary's Academy. When she graduated three years later, she accepted a job as a seamstress in a factory, but she felt making hundreds of pockets for pants was not her calling. Her next position was as a waitress in the Colonial, located in the French Quarter. This job was a radical move, as nice girls did not frequent the area, a red-light district. The experience led to her realization that her heart lay with food, both for her own enjoyment and for the joy of others. Leah was likewise smitten with the environment of white tablecloths and flatware, a novel experience, as the city did not have sit-down restaurants for African-Americans.

At a 1945 Mardi Gras ball, Leah caught the attention of Edgar "Dooky" Chase II, five years younger, a bandleader who coaxed the cadence of jazz from his trumpet. In 1946, the couple married in secret; although Edgar had the parental requirements of being Catholic and Creole, her parents considered musicians financially unstable. Leah hated the nomadic life of travelling with his band, and when the first of their four children arrived, she felt justified in being a stay-at-home mother. Around 1952, with Edgar's father's health declining, the son stepped in to run Dooky Chase, the family's street corner stand, which sold lottery tickets and where black workers could cash their paychecks. Its locale was Tremé, one of the nation's oldest African-American neighborhoods, and its menu consisted of po' boy sandwiches, crusty loaves of bread stuffed with chaurice—spicy pork sausages—or fried oysters. When the children attended school full-time, Mrs. Chase wanted to bring fine dining to her community and worked alongside her husband. Over time, the stand evolved into Dooky Chase Restaurant. In an echo of the Colonial, Leah introduced fancy fare such as Lobster Thermidor and shrimp cocktail. However, when her customers thought shrimp cocktail was an alcoholic beverage, she switched to the familiar Creole cuisine. Her dishes belong to a deeply rooted New Orleans tradition that combines the products of the Louisiana countryside, the bayous, and the marshes with sophisticated cooking techniques from the kitchens of West Africa, France, and Spain. The revised menu proved to be a success, and the restaurant grew in stature until it became a local landmark and the destination for top black entertainers. The ninety-five-year-old Mrs. Chase remembers each performer's preference: Nat King Cole, four-minute eggs; Lena Horne, fried chicken; Duke Ellington, gumbo; Cicely Tyson, crab meat. Ray Charles immortalized the eatery in popular lore when he recorded "Early in the Morning Blues" and improvised the lyric, "I went to Dooky Chase to get something to eat. The waitress looked at me and said, 'Ray, you sure look beat.'"

Part of the charm of Dooky Chase is in its ties to the civil rights movement. Although Jim Crow laws had forbidden the races to mix in public, city officials had turned the other way in the case of this restaurant, fearful of the public outcry if they tried to intervene with the beloved eatery. The Chases provided a private room at the top of the stairs for clandestine meetings for black voter-registration campaign organizers, the NAACP, and campus sit-ins. Among those who gathered there were Thurgood Marshall and Martin Luther King, Sr., who Leah nicknamed Big Daddy King. Nothing could stop the couple from feeding the movement: not threatening letters, not a pipe bomb, not fear of arrest. When the Freedom Riders were behind bars, Mrs. Chase delivered take-out. Leah recalled, "I feel like in this restaurant we changed the course of the world over bowls of gumbo. That's how we always did the planning—over gumbo." In a foodie town, vittles heal wounds.

In New Orleans, a city that reveres its cafes as civic monuments the way New York City reveres the Statue of Liberty or San Francisco the Golden Gate Bridge, Dooky Chase is an emporium that serves nearly two hundred people at a time. Leah has an appreciation for forms of artistic expression other than food, and the restaurant's violet and cream walls display canvases of mid- and late twentieth-century African-American art. Behind the buffet line, stained glass panels depict New Orleans street and market scenes. The reason for her patronage is to help others, and for selfish reasons as well. Leah explained, "I could be as mean as a sack of rattlesnakes if I didn't have this art to soften me up." Indeed, when people do not meet her exacting standards, she uses the expression "stupid jackass." After years of collecting canvasses, Leah became the subject of one. A painting of Mrs. Chase wearing her trademark pink baseball cap, absorbed in slicing yellow squash, has been added to the collection of iconic American images in the National Portrait Gallery, part of the Smithsonian in Washington, DC, under the same roof as presidential portraits ranging from George Washington to Barack Obama. When the artist asked whether she thought the rendition accurate, the eighty-nine-year-old Leah responded, "You could have made me look like Halle Berry or Lena Horne, but you made it look like me." Signs of Leah's faith also decorate the walls. Above the kitchen doorway is an assortment of crucifixes that a regular customer brings back from his travels and presents as a tribute. A birthday blessing from Pope Benedict hangs nearby, alongside a framed photograph of Pope Francis, a gift from a nun.

Dooky Chase is a mecca for meals because of its spicy delicacies, and it remains a political meeting ground where the city's leaders, black and white, settle problems over plates of steaming crawfish, paneed rabbit, or seafood jambalaya. President George H. W. Bush had quail and grits the last time he was there; another guest was presidential candidate Barack Obama, whom Leah chastised for putting hot sauce on her famed gumbo.

The wrath of nature came to call when Hurricane Katrina struck in 2005, soaking the eatery with five feet of water and forcing Dooky and Leah to move into a FEMA trailer across the street from their restaurant. Looters capitalized on the calamity and raided all its liquor, the payroll, the cash registers—everything but the art collection. The rebuilding effort moved slowly, in part because Mr. Chase did not like to borrow money in much the same way as he hated to spend it. Mrs. Chase said of her spouse, "He wouldn't give a crippled crab a crutch to get to a gumbo party."

Alas, one does not reach age ninety-five without experiencing pain, and Leah had her share of vicissitudes. In the early days of the restaurant, Mrs. Chase kept a three-gallon vat of boiling water steeped in tea on a shelf, and it was accidentally poured on her in a scalding cascade. Her doctor placed bandages all over her blister-covered body, making her resemble a mummy, yet she did not miss a day of work. Another burn occurred when she was cleaning her grill; she recalled, "But you keep going. You put a little powder on your face and you keep going." A tragedy that would have tested someone with less faith was losing her daughter Emily, who died giving birth to her seventh child. The baby only survived for several months. Leah did not take time off to grieve; her staff and customers depended on her. In 2016, her husband of seventy-one years passed away. Although they had often had problem patches in their marriage, Dooky was the love of her life. What helps her keep going are three children, sixteen grandchildren, and twenty-six great-grandchildren.

Despite her being almost a century old, it is a given in New Orleans that one will always find Leah Chase in the kitchen of her restaurant, chopping vegetables or stewing chicken before lunch service, clad in a shocking pink chef's uniform—she said she gave up white because, at her age, she needed more color in her life—or in the dining room, greeting everyone from cufflink-clad bankers to guidebook-toting tourists. Nearing the century mark, when most of her peers have contentedly gone "out to pasture"—or at least to sip sweetened tea in the shade of a magnolia tree—she shows no signs of becoming a "tin-tin" (Creole for a retired little old lady). As the grande dame of Creole cooking says, "Seven days a week, yes, indeed. And no, I don't know myself where I get the energy, I get up in the morning, say a little prayer, 'Lord, get me through this day,' and then I get through it." No waitress ever needed to tell her, "Leah, you sure look beat." The reason for her refusal to step down is that she loves the way she spends her time, and, as she explained, "Everybody on this earth is obligated to do something to make it better. This is what I'm doing."

Over the years, there has been an outpouring of Hails to the Chef, and one is *Leah Chase: Listen, I Say Like This*. The title is an allusion to the expression utilized by elderly Creoles when they wish to emphasize a point. Leah dedicated the book to her late daughter. Cicely Tyson gave Mrs. Chase a t-shirt with this slogan emblazoned on the front. The autobiography is replete with photographs of Chase and celebrity customers: Julia Child, Jesse Jackson, Dizzy Gillespie, Bryant Gumbel, Quincy Jones. The indefatigable Mrs. Chase became the first black recipient of the James Beard Foundation's Lifetime Achievement Award. Leah also received the unlikely chef accolades of serving as the inspiration for Tiana in *The Princess and the Frog*, Disney's first African-American princess, and starring in Beyoncé's "Lemonade" video.

Because of Dooky Chase's association with fighters for racial equality, tantalizing cuisine, and her iconic status as Queen of Creole, one can easily find oneself humming the old Southern lyric, "I wish I was in Dixie, hooray! Hooray!"

CHAPTER FOURTEEN

Bon Appétit (1924)

The word celebrity used to belong to the provenance of
famous musicians, actors, and athletes. It later embraced
celebrity chefs, the gourmets who produce Pavlovian
responses in dedicated foodies. However, what has been
relegated to the shadows is the female Francophile
responsible for taking cooks out of the closet and into
the mainstream.

As a child, Judith Bailey would gladly have preferred,
had they existed in the 1930s, an Easy-Bake oven over any
number of Barbies. She was born with a sophisticated palate,
one not satiated in her Manhattan home, where meals were
products of the Depression and wartime cooking. Her mother,
Phyllis, ordered groceries by telephone, and dinners consisted
of English-style meat and boiled potatoes. Mrs. Bailey
prohibited the purchase of garlic, as she considered it vulgar,
and likewise felt that conversation regarding food was as
crude as discussing sex. To satisfy her culinary craving, Judith
took refuge in the kitchen with the family cook. At the child's
urging, the cook described the food from her native Barbados:
exotic fruits, hot peppers that made one sweat, and the
Baileys' "forbidden fruit"—garlic. Her attorney father, Charles,
indulged her with Saturday visits to a French restaurant.

Judith attended the Brearley School in New York City
and Bennington College in Vermont, where she graduated in
1945 with a degree in her other main interest, English. She
obtained an assistant editorial position with Doubleday,
where she worked for three years. At that juncture, she
persuaded her frugal father to finance a three-week trip to

Paris, a city that had always beckoned. A few days before she had to return to the States, she left her purse on a bench in the Tuileries; without a passport or return ticket, she had to extend her stay. Penniless, she was desperately seeking work when she happened to overhear another American speaking, on the phone in her hotel's lobby, to someone from *Weekend* magazine, a publication aimed at American tourists. Ironically, on the other end of the line was the editor of *Weekend*, the very person Judith had been futilely trying to contact. She grabbed the phone and spoke to Evan Jones.

Mr. Jones and Ms. Bailey not only fell in love, but they also helped each other discover the joy of French cuisine. Judith's letters to her parents waxed poetic about her American boyfriend, with whom she shared an apartment that they had turned into "a speakeasy restaurant." In one letter, she wrote, "I know you didn't send me to an expensive college to have me become a cook. But you must understand that in France, cooking is not regarded as demeaning. It is an art." The Baileys were not impressed with her cooking or her cohabitation.

Despite parental censure, Judith had the time of her life. Too poor to be regulars at the three-star restaurants, the couple enjoyed *boudin blanc* at a local café, shopped for ingredients, and perfected their French. Unable to support herself on love and food alone, in 1950 she obtained a job in Doubleday's Paris office, where the twenty-seven-year-old's task was to file rejected submissions. In a 2001 interview with the Associated Press, she recounted, "One day my boss said, 'Oh, will you get rid of these books and write some letters of rejection.' He went off to have some lunch with some French publishers. I curled up with one or two books. I was just curious. I think it was the face on the cover. I looked at that face and I started reading that book and I didn't stop all afternoon. I was in tears when my boss came back. I said, 'This book is going to New York and has got to be published.' And he said, 'What? That book by that kid?'" *Anne Frank: The Diary of a Young Girl* became an international sensation, one of the best-selling books of all time. Judith shrugged off accolades and merely claimed to have been in the right place at the right time.

Judith and Evan were married in 1951 in Vienna; she became the stepmother to his two daughters, and the couple adopted two children of their own. The Joneses settled in New York, where they did their best to replicate the food of France. However, finding ingredients, or even an omelet pan, proved difficult. American cookbooks were equally discouraging. In that era, most American recipes required a can opener, and baking instructions were available on the backs of boxes. Mrs. Jones later wrote, "The prevailing message was that the poor little woman didn't have time to cook, and, moreover, it was beneath her dignity." To their mutual disgust, America lived under the dominion of Swanson's frozen dinners, a staple that included the essential food groups, though devoid of nutritional value. Judith found the bread in Manhattan so tasteless that she baked her own. Meals, prepared in husband-and-wife tandem, led critic Stanley Kauffmann to describe their East Sixty-Sixth Street apartment as "the best restaurant in New York."

Because of her acclaim for *The Diary of Anne Frank*, Alfred A. Knopf hired Judith in 1957, not a typical '50s stay-at-home mother, as a junior editor. She started off primarily as a translator of French writers such as Jean-Paul Sartre and Albert Camus, as well as English literary lions John Updike, Anne Tyler, and John Hershey, which aligned with her love of literature. Publishing lore holds that she wielded her green editing pencil like a knife. And, one day, on her desk landed a submission that involved her other great love. Judith Jones was again "in the right place at the right time."

A decade after she brought to light the world's most famous diary, a shopworn eight-hundred-page manuscript, by three unknown women with no literary credentials, appeared on her desk. Several editors had rejected the book as overly long, and it had the uninspired title *French Recipes for American Cooks.* Judith was intrigued by its chief writer, who she felt was a kindred spirit: Both were die-hard French foodies who had fallen in love with their American husbands in Paris. (One difference: Julia Child was six foot two, and Judith Jones was described as a waif). Judith wrote of the book's discovery, "From the moment I started turning its pages I was *bouleversee,* as the French say, 'knocked out.'" She took it home and tried some of the recipes, and they proved a love connection. The cookbook's appeal was that it took the mystery out of *coq au vin* and *boeuf bourguignon* and hundreds of other dishes long believed too daunting for the American cook. Although she was still too junior to make a pitch to her editor, Jones was astute enough to realize it was the book she had been searching for; she renamed it *Mastering the Art of French Cooking.* When she showed the revised title to Mr. Knopf, he scowled and said, "Well, I'll eat my hat if that title sells." In her memoir, *The Tenth Muse,* Judith responded, "I like to think of all the hats he had to eat." Jones was convinced that, if the cookbook was something she needed to replicate the taste of France in America, others would feel the same. In 1961, with its release, Mrs. Jones envisioned what others could not: that cooking was an art and that chef celebrities would one day be lionized.

The classic cookbook sold more than a million copies and shifted the culinary landscape of a country raised on canned vegetables. It also launched Child on a long-running public-television career as host of *The French Chef.* In 2009, the book received a resurgence of interest due to the book and movie *Julie & Julia* (Erin Dilly played Mrs. Jones, and Meryl Streep played Mrs. Child.) Encouraged, Judith changed her editorial roster to dealing exclusively with culinary writers. Jones had a long-standing interest in regional American writers such as Edna Lewis, the granddaughter of a former slave. The eventual book, *The Taste of Country Cooking,* required Mrs. Jones to cull through Edna's notes, penned on a yellow legal pad, one page at a time. Another of her authors was Joan

Nathan, an eminent Jewish-cooking authority, who travelled with Judith to Israel while working on *The Foods of Israel Today.* Joan recalled that Judith was exacting, and when the editor "put a green 'nice' on anything you had written, you would fly through the sky." Marion Cunningham, another client, reminisced about the time she went to Mrs. Jones's Episcopal Church. Cunningham was a lapsed Catholic, but she was still mindful that Catholics should take communion only from a Catholic priest. Once communion commenced, Judith had turned to Marion and told her to go up and take communion with her. Marion had to decide who she was more afraid of, God or Judith Jones. She took communion. Jones turned her roster of writers into stars at a time when home cooking and those who practiced it were looked down on in a male-dominated publishing world. Ruth Reichl of *Gourmet* magazine says, "Food started getting serious respect largely because of her. When you talk about the cookbook revolution, she *was* the revolution."

At age seventy-two, Judith lost her best friend, her husband, Evan, who died from injuries sustained in their Manhattan home. Even then, the grieving widow was determined not to let his absence deter her from continuing their favorite ritual. From this experience came her book, *The Pleasures of Cooking for One.* Her cookbook was a blend of kitchen advice and encouragement for people who live alone in their final years. Julia Moskin wrote in the *Times,* "Mrs. Jones is an evangelist for the psychic, spiritual, physical, and intellectual benefits cooking can bring old people: the math and concentration required for following a recipe, the exercise of kneading bread or whisking eggs, the self-regard that shows in setting a place and sitting down for a meal."

Two years later, Jones wrote *The Tenth Muse: My Life in Food* (the allusion in the title is to the French epicure and gastronome Brillat-Savarin, who wrote of the tenth muse, Gasterea, goddess of the pleasures of taste). In the memoir, Judith shared many of her coveted recipes. Her final book,

Love Me, Feed Me, a guide to making food that a cook could share with a dog (hers was named Mabon), was penned at age ninety. Her writing included anecdotes from her life, many from her rural summer home, Ryn Teg Farm, in Walden Township, Vermont. One story entailed skinning, brining, and frying the tail of a beaver that had been causing a nuisance.

At a discussion group in a bookstore in Washington, Judith quoted an old Italian saying, "At the table, one never grows old. Isn't that enough reason to come home at the end of the day, roll up one's sleeves, fire up the stove, and start smashing the garlic?" Where Jones came home from at the end of the day was Knopf; she retired after half a century at age eighty-nine. Reminiscing over her long career, she said that what had irked her for many years was when people assumed she was a secretary, rather than an editor.

Judith Jones passed away in Walden at age ninety-three from complications of Alzheimer's. Tributes poured in for the woman who gave the world *The Diary of a Young Girl* and *Mastering the Art of French Cooking*, and who illustrated that eating alone need not be a lonely endeavor. She deserves a posthumous toast—from a bottle of French wine—with Julia Child's sign-off words from *The French Chef*: "*Bon appétit!*"

CHAPTER FIFTEEN

Geraniums (1925)

Portia, in William Shakespeare's *The Merchant of Venice*, says, "How far that little candle throws his beams! So shines a good deed in a naughty world." This metaphor holds true in the case of an elderly female David who fought a Goliath. Battling injustice until her eighth decade, this woman could not stop while there were still dragons to slay.

Parents read to their children to instill the love of books, to entertain, to bond. In Helen Balmuth's case, the tales did not end with a happily-ever-after. She was the daughter of Louis, a father who had endured pogrom-ridden Poland; though he immigrated to Britain at age nine, anti-Semitism had left an imprint on his soul. In his late thirties, in an arranged wedding, he married Marie Bader, the daughter of Polish parents. Their union was unhappy, as Marie was disappointed by her acrimonious spouse and their poverty. While she hoped Helen would fulfill her own aborted dream and become a socialite, Louis instilled in his only child a sense of social activism. As World War II ravaged Europe, he religiously listened to broadcasts by Goebbels and read excerpts from Hitler's *Mein Kampf (My Struggle)*, explaining that the book was a blueprint for their genocide. Home in the working-class neighborhood of Amhurst Park, filled with a sense of impending doom, instilled in the little girl a feeling of insecurity. Helen, a sickly child (probably due to a bout of tuberculosis), secluded herself in her room to dodge her parents' violent quarrels. On one occasion, Helen came home and, discovering her mother and father had gone out, fantasized that they were dead. The only ray of light came from her beloved Aunt Mina, who dyed her hair platinum, sported ritzy homemade clothes, and had a boyfriend and spares. She perished in the Café de Paris during the Blitz of 1941. Following the tragedy, a panic-stricken Louis evacuated his family to the countryside. Helen recalled, "I was well aware that we would be annihilated. By the time I was ten, I knew it all."

In her late teens, Helen worked as a secretary for the National Association of Mental Health, which treated veterans, and in 1945, she defied her mother and volunteered for the Jewish Relief Unit sent by the UN to work with Holocaust survivors. The nineteen-year-old trekked across a new European landscape, where forty million people were adrift. Her training had entailed dealing with misery, but nothing prepared her for the "gray ghosts at the doorway of the world," as one of her fellow workers described the displaced. They ended up in the Bergen-Belsen concentration camp, where more than fifty thousand people—including Anne Frank and her sister Margot—had died, and where the British liberators discovered thirteen thousand corpses. Relief workers distributed food and clothing to twelve thousand survivors housed in nearby barracks. Many of the victims had perished from typhus, and Helen forever remembered the cloying smell that pervaded the unhallowed ground. As she stared at the result of the inhumanity man had inflicted on man, she saw the world as divided into two camps: bystanders and witnesses. At first, she felt helpless in the face of a tsunami of suffering, but gradually realized that, though she could not change the survivors' reality, she could listen. Helen explained, "People wanted to tell their story and I was able to receive it. They would hold me and dig their fingers in and rasp this story out..They would rock back and forth, and I would say to them, 'I will tell your story. Your story will not die.' It took me a long time to realize that that was all I could do." The eighteen months she spent in Germany would shape the rest of Helen's life; she would never be a bystander.

Shortly after her return to Britain, Helen attended a New Year's Eve party where she met Rudi Bamberger, who had anglicized his name to the more British-sounding Bamber, and she moved with him to a condemned apartment. His mother had met her end in a concentration camp, and Nazis had beaten his father to death in Nuremberg on Kristallnacht. Rudi had survived the war, yet could not escape his demons. Although they loved one another, their marriage soon developed fissures. Like her father, Rudi was a pessimist, drowning in his own darkness, and Helen, not wanting the same lot in life as her mother, divorced him after twenty-three years. She explained that living with victims is a very different matter from working with them, and added that it would have been easier if they had simply not liked each other. They remained friends until he died, but "I was sad for a long time; I think I'm still sad."

Life was tough after they split up, and Helen worked to support her sons, Jonathan and David. However, in some ways, the marital breakdown was liberating. She rented out rooms to foreign students who filled the house with laughter, something that had not existed in her parents' home or the one she had shared with Rudi. Helen stated that she had always felt sorry for her parents and was determined that would not be how people viewed her.

After meeting Anna Freud, she worked with the Jewish Refugee Committee and helped look after the more than seven hundred orphans who had been at Auschwitz-Birkenau. In her role as a counselor, she recalled "their stony little faces, giving nothing back, their skeptical eyes—a complete lack of trust." Helen found she could establish a connection by persuading them to reconnect with their pre-war memories. A harder task was to find schools willing to take the youngsters on in a post-war Britain preoccupied with its own problems. Mrs. Bamber remembered a promising young refugee who applied to an elite school, but, understandably, was deficient in academics. One headmaster scoffed, "Didn't they give them any books to read in those camps?"

Horrified by accounts of the use of torture by the French in Algeria, Bamber joined Amnesty International, an organization formed in 1961 to publicize the plight of prisoners of conscience, and rose to be chairwoman of the British branch. In Latin America, she worked with the "disappeared" and tortured in Chile, Argentina, and Nicaragua. Over the next three decades, like the fictional Tom Joad, wherever there was an injustice, Helen was there.

She and others left Amnesty International to branch out on their own, and at age sixty, a time when most people are slowing down, Mrs. Bamber established the Medical Foundation for the Care of Victims of Torture (now Freedom from Torture). They wanted to go beyond documenting abuses to treating them, using many of the methods she had learned at Bergen-Belsen. A grant from the United Nations Voluntary Fund provided initial funds, and the Foundation operated out of two rooms at the National Temperance Hospital in London, where she had one part-time assistant and a typewriter. She draped a cloth over the single mirror because many of her patients were too damaged to bear their reflections. From this humble inception, the center grew to a staff of more than 100 professions dealing with more than fifty thousand people from more than ninety countries, including Bosnia, Chile, Congo, Iran, Rwanda, and Sri Lanka. In her quest to bring succor, Helen travelled to many of these geographical landmines. Most visitors were taken aback by the Center's ministering angel; she stood four feet ten inches and compensated with towering heels; she sported permed hair, nail polish, and scarlet lipstick. Somehow, despite her advanced age and hard life, the light in her eyes remained undiminished. Anne Frank's words were true to Helen's spirit: "In spite of everything I still believe that people are really good at heart."

In 1993, approaching her seventies, Mrs. Bamber took on an excruciatingly painful task when she went to Israel and testified on behalf of a Palestinian prisoner who had confessed, under torture by the Israeli security forces, of being a member of Hamas. In her attempt to understand his pain, she sat for an hour wearing a hood like the one officers had put over prisoners' heads during interrogations. She said she gagged and felt a rising sense of panic. The experience was Bamber's variation of Sophie's Choice: to accuse Israel, the state founded by her fellow Jews, of torture. Afterward, a man came up to her and spat out his contempt: "With friends like you, who needs enemies?" Although accused of being a Judas, she felt she had to confront injustice, regardless of the perpetrator.

Helen remained at the helm of the organization for almost twenty years. In 2005, tireless at eighty, she and Michael Korzinski began the Helen Bamber Foundation. It included not only torture survivors, but also those who had suffered other forms of human right violations, including those brutalized by criminal gangs, trafficked for work or sex, or used as slaves. Through a holistic combination of medicine and psychological, social, and physical therapies, Bamber's organization helped torture victims recover from unspeakable horrors: electric shocks to genitals, beatings on the bottoms of the feet, nonlethal hangings. At age eighty-three, Mrs. Bamber continued to work every morning, including weekends, the time when she met the most psychologically traumatized people.

The efforts of the diminutive woman who cast a giant shadow garnered recognition and respect. The former president of the European Court of Human Rights, Sir Nicolas Bratza, described her as "a formidable force of nature who earned and commanded the respect of all who had the good fortune to meet her." Mrs. Bamber advised Colin Firth on his role in *The Railway Man*, a 2013 movie based on the British soldier Eric Lomax, who was captured by the Japanese during

World War II and forced to work on the Thai-Burma railway, known as the "death railway" because of the thousands of prisoners who perished during its construction. Firth said that, even in old age and ill health, Helen continued to be determined to do all she could to help those affected by evil. Lomax became a client of the medical foundation in the late 1980s and called Helen a pivotal figure in his late-in-life rehabilitation. In 1993, Helen was honored with the European Women of Achievement Award, and in 1997, she was admitted to the Order of the British Empire. She held honorary degrees from Oxford, Glasgow, Ulster, and several other universities.

Despite the accolades, a miasma of self-reproof lingered, stemming from the sorrow that, though she saved thousands, she could not save her relationship with Rudi. In addition to this heartache, Helen had a complicated relationship with her sons, who harbored a sense of resentment that she had been more motherly to thousands of the dispossessed than she had been to them. Helen lived alone in an apartment where few visited; she had spent her life in the pursuit of justice at the expense of cultivating personal relationships. Most evenings were spent at her foundation and ended with her team gathering in her office for a bottle of wine. Often, they dropped by the local Thai restaurant, where the owners always brought a cushion for her to sit on. "Sometimes," she said, "we go mad and try Greek."

In Neil Belton's 2012 biography *The Good Listener,* the author described how Helen, the consummate humanitarian, kept geraniums in pots on the terrace of her London apartment. When she crushed their petals, she remembered, in Proustian fashion, the cloying scent of death in Belsen. She explained that she did so because of "the need to forget, the wish to remember."

CHAPTER SIXTEEN

78651 (1927)

In his self-appointed role as an avenging angel, Holocaust survivor Simon Wiesenthal meted out retribution to the Nazis for their crimes against humanity. In contrast, another victim of the Holocaust set her eyes to the future rather than the past and dedicated her life to reconciliation, which she felt was the best salve for her fractured France.

The journalist Agnes Poirier recalled an afternoon in 2008 when she saw France's most revered feminist for the last time. Poirier was in a café when an old man asked its patrons to stand with the words, "We are paying tribute to the deported. Today is the anniversary of the liberation of Auschwitz." His request was in reference to a group of concentration camp survivors, parading down the street, carrying the French flag. Holding the tri-color symbolized their forgiveness of the nation that had betrayed them. In their midst was an eighty-one-year-old woman, the conscience of her country.

Simone Annie Jacob, born in Nice on the French Riviera, was the youngest of the four children of Yvonne and Andre Jacob, non-observant Jews. Simone did not pay much attention to her religion until the swastika flew from the Eiffel Tower and the Vichy regime expelled her father from his profession as an architect. The day before her arrest by the Gestapo, the teenaged Simone had completed her baccalaureate, the diploma required to pursue university studies. Simone, her eldest sibling, Madeleine (nicknamed Milou), and their mother were deported to Drancy, the transit camp, followed by evacuation to Auschwitz-Birkenau. Her sister Denise, who had entered the Resistance at the start of the War, ended up in Ravensbrück; her father and brother—last recorded in Lithuania on a convoy of French Jews bound for Estonia—were never heard from again. In a preface to a book about the Holocaust, Simone wrote, "I found myself thrown into a universe of death, humiliation, and barbarism. I am still haunted by the images, the odors, the screams, the humiliation, the blows, and the sky, ashen with the smoke from the crematoriums." When she entered through the iron gate, in a stroke of fortune, a woman who helped run the camp was taken with the teen with the beautiful chestnut braids, and told her in broken French, "You are too pretty to die here. I am going to find some way so you can survive." Her savior sent Simone, her mother, and her sister to work at a Siemens factory outside the barbed wire, and later, a position in an SS kitchen enabled her to pilfer food. The three women ended up in Bergen-Belsen, where Yvonne languished from typhus until she succumbed, shortly before the camp's liberation. Of the seventy-five thousand Jews deported from France, the sisters were two of only 2,500 to return. In 2005, Simone explained her survival to an interviewer: "I'm often asked what gave me the strength and will to continue to fight. I believe deeply that it was my mother; she has never stopped being present to me, next to me."

Anxious to rebuild her life, Simone resumed her studies, including law at the Institut d'Etudes Politiques in Paris, where she met a fellow student, Antoine Veil. They married in 1946 and had three sons, Jean, Claude-Nicolas, and Pierre-Francois. Despite the demands of her family, Simone focused on her career as a lawyer and passed the extremely competitive national examination to become a magistrate. As an official in the Justice Ministry, she focused on improving the living conditions of prisoners and the mentally ill, two groups targeted by the Nazis. The story went that when Valery Giscard d'Estaing became president, he visited Antoine Veil, a civil servant who had become a powerful figure in the aeronautical industry, to invite him to join the government. As it transpired, the President ended up choosing forty-six-year-old Simone for the position, making her the second woman to hold full cabinet rank. Soon she was advising ministers (including Francois Mitterrand) and was involved in the case of Djamila Bouhired, a young woman raped with a bottle in an Algerian prison, who Simone brought to safety in France.

Under President Giscard d'Estaing's leadership, Mrs. Veil spoke out on behalf of victims of communist oppression in the Soviet Union, Latin America, and Vietnam. The most inflammatory act of her career involved the legalization of abortion, a procedure that had been criminalized since the Napoleonic Era. Another Simone (de Beauvoir) had previously paved the way with the 1949 publication of *The Second Sex*, a thousand-page book that strongly advocated for the right of women to control their own bodies. Unlike the writer, Veil did not campaign for the legalization out of ideology, but out of humanism. She could not bear the thought that those burdened with an unwanted pregnancy were compelled to travel, either to Switzerland or to England, or to face the horror of resorting to an unlicensed abortionist. In 1974, wearing a blue dress and a string of pearls, the forty-seven-year-old Veil addressed the French National Assembly with the words, "I will share a conviction of women, and I apologize for doing it in front of this assembly comprised almost exclusively of men. No women resort to abortion lightheartedly." In a calm and determined voice, she pointed out that two hundred thousand French women were suffering from the effects of clandestine abortions each year, and that it was time to end such suffering. After three days of acrimonious debate, the government passed the "Loi Veil" by a vote of 284 to 189. During this time, the chamber had resonated with epithets such as "act of murder," "monstrous," and "France is making coffins instead of cribs." Her critics likened abortion to Nazi euthanasia; one asked, "Madame Minister, do you want to send children to the ovens?" Madame Minister wept as she heard these words. She later attacked the rampant hypocrisy, pointing out that many who opposed her measure were simultaneously arranging abortions for a mistress or for a loved one. More than thirty years later, Simone still received hate mail. She admitted having faced challenges as a woman involved in civic affairs, and referred to political parties in France as "men's clubs." In a firm voice, she added that being female in an authoritarian role was precarious "because the very thing people admire in men becomes a point of criticism in women."

Mrs. Veil left the government in 1979 and became the first female president of the European Parliament, a precursor to the European Union that promoted continental unity, a position she held until 1982. The august title made her one of the highest-ranking elected women in the world, along with Prime Ministers Margaret Thatcher of Britain and Indira Gandhi of India. Simone viewed her election as a symbol of hope: "If this Parliament has a Jew, a woman, for its president, it means everyone has the same rights. That means a lot to me." Her platform was the reconciliation of Germany with the countries it had occupied. Afterward, she returned to politics and served as the Minister of Health, Social Affairs, and Urban Issues until age sixty-eight. Unwilling to retire, she became president of the High Council for Integration, a body devoted to the assimilation of immigrants, and in 1998, she began a nine-year term as a member of the Constitutional Council, the country's highest legal authority. Mrs. Veil also served as the president of the *Fondation pour la Memoire de la Shoah*, France's Holocaust remembrance organization, from which she represented the dwindling number of survivors and helped to keep the flame of remembrance lit. From 2003 to 2009, Veil was chairman of the board of the Trust Fund for Victims, a group that supports survivors of genocide, war crimes, and crimes against humanity in cooperation with the International Criminal Court. In 2005, Simone returned to Auschwitz to commemorate the sixtieth anniversary of its liberation. Simone was devastated by the death of her sister Milou in a car accident in 1952 and the passing of her middle son in 2002. In 2013, Simone suffered a dual blow with the deaths of her sister Denise and her husband, Antoine. Her sixty-seven-year marriage had provided the strength to withstand the loss of her loved ones and the trauma of her past.

Indefatigable into her eighties, the humanitarian took time from her innumerable pursuits to publish her 2017 autobiography in which she criticized the long delay in the government's acceptance of responsibility for the murder of its Jews. After decades of denial, the French state admitted its collective guilt for the crimes in 1995. The tireless crusader was similar to the Roman God Janus (from whom we derive the name for January), whose image depicted two profiles: One turned to the left to represent the past, while the other turned to the right to represent the future. Robert Badinter, a former justice minister and Holocaust survivor, in an article in the *Guardian*, wrote that the politician, although always aware of yesterday, turned her eyes to tomorrow. He recalled that when the "Butcher of Lyons," Klaus Barbie, was on trial in the late 1980s for war crimes, Veil did not approve. She explained that she was not interested in stirring up the pain of yesterday, and that Vichy and the collaboration had not represented France. This stance was especially noble given that she had been the victim of post-war denial. In 1950, at a reception hosted by the French consulate in Mainz, Germany, a French diplomat asked Simone if her tattoo was her cloakroom number. The callous remark caused her to burst into tears. In admiration, Badinter wrote, "Simone had a *"qualité d'âme*, a nobility of the soul, which is very rare."

When Simone Veil passed away in 2017 at age eighty-nine, President Macron stood before her flag-draped coffin at the center of the Invalides courtyard in the shadow of Napoleon's tomb. The inscription above the entrance of the ancient monument is "To great men, a grateful country." He addressed the great lady lying in state, saying, "You have, Madame, made our old nation better and more beautiful. Your grandeur is ours. As you are leaving us, will you please,

Madame, accept the French people's deepest gratitude."
Holocaust survivors, politicians, and dignitaries, as well
as Simone's two surviving sons, were in attendance at the
ceremony. Pierre- Francois Veil, an attorney, spoke about
his mother, saying, "This tribute is your ultimate victory on
the death camps." Macron announced that the First Lady of
France would be laid to rest in the Paris Pantheon, a structure
whose imposing dome overlooks the Fifth Arrondissement of
Paris. Of the eighty interred there, Mrs. Veil became the fifth
woman; Antoine was moved from his cemetery to lie once
more beside his wife. Others selected for interment in the
sacred mausoleum are Voltaire, Victor Hugo, Rousseau, and
Emile Zola. Another, to whom Simone would relate, was Jean
Moulin, a leader of the French Resistance.

Before this great honor, Simone had received another
laurel when the Académie Française, the elite intellectual
guardians of the French language, founded in the seventeenth
century, inducted her into their distinguished body. This
honor made her the sixth woman of the forty "immortals,"
the name given to its members. Each of the recipients, clad
in a green uniform (Karl Lagerfeld of Chanel designed hers),
receives a ceremonial sword. Inscribed on Simone's were the
three phrases that could serve as her encapsulated biography:
the motto of the French Republic: *"Liberté, Égalité, Fraternité"*;
the European Union's *"Unie dans la diversité"*; and the number
tattooed on her arm: 78651.

CHAPTER SEVENTEEN

Mr. Bojangles (1928)

F. Scott Fitzgerald wrote, "There are no second acts in American lives." His words proved a self-fulfilling prophecy when the hand that penned *The Great Gatsby* shook so much from alcoholic tremors that he could no longer hold a pen. In contrast, other artists have reinvented themselves in their later years, a fact demonstrated by a woman who proved there was life after "The Good Ship Lollipop."

Having given birth to two boys, Shirley's mother, Gertrude, longed for a daughter, one who would be the dancer she had aspired to be. In 1927, her father, George, had his tonsils removed because a doctor suggested it might improve his chances of siring a girl. Ten months later, Shirley Jane Temple was born in Santa Monica, California. By the age of three, for fifty cents a week, she was taking classes at Ethel Meglin's (a Ziegfeld Follies alumna) Dance Studio in Hollywood, where a fellow student was nine-year-old Judy Garland. When a talent scout chose Shirley and eleven other toddlers to star in *Baby Burlesks*, a series of suggestive one-reel shorts—shades of the future *Toddlers & Tiaras*—in which Temple imitated Marlene Dietrich, Mae West, and Dolores del Rio, he launched the career of one of the silver screen's immortal stars. The producers locked any child who misbehaved in a windowless room with only a block of ice as a seat. Before each performance, Gertrude trilled, "Sparkle, Shirley, sparkle!"

Shirley's career really began in 1934, when she starred in *Stand Up and Cheer*, one of the many films made during a decade in which music chased away an unhappy reality:

America was in the grip of the Great Depression, and the
Nazis had goose-stepped into the Rhineland. Within an hour
of her completing her song-and-dance number "Baby, Take a
Bow," Fox Studios placed her under contract for a year at $150
a week. Other roles followed, such as *The Little Colonel, Heidi,*
and *Wee Willie Winkie;* the world was gaga for the tot with the
corkscrew curls styled in imitation of silent-film star Mary
Pickford. Temple later explained the adoration: "People in the
Depression wanted something to cheer them up, and they
fell in love with a dog, Rin Tin Tin, and a little girl." President
Franklin D. Roosevelt proclaimed, "As long as our country has
Shirley Temple, we will be all right." Yet there was a downside
to fame. Ms. Temple stopped believing in Santa Claus at
age six when her mother took her to see Kris Kringle in a
department store, and he asked for her autograph.

Shirley's fan mail averaged sixteen thousand letters a
month, more than arrived for Greta Garbo. Princess Elizabeth
and Princess Margaret were among her admirers. Her
birthday brought 167,000 presents, all of which her parents
gave to charity. Not only were mothers (like Shirley MacLaine)
naming their little girls after the starlet, they dressed them
in S. T. fashion, bought look-alike dolls (now collector's items),
and coiled their hair in her trademark ringlets. One mother
even offered George a stud fee in the hope he would sire
another Shirley.

As one of the most successful child stars of the cinema,
Temple grew up coloring with Gary Cooper and playing
croquet with Orson Welles. She based her comfort with adults
on the softness of their laps and later remarked that J. Edgar
Hoover's was the most comfortable. One of the few spankings
Shirley received from her father followed a barbeque given
by Eleanor Roosevelt at Hyde Park. When her hostess bent
down to put chops on the barbeque, the mischievous ten-
year-old took aim with her slingshot and landed a pebble
smack on the First Lady's rump. She learned geography
by tracking her friend Amelia Earhart's flights and learned

about racial prejudice in Palm Springs. She had a lavish suite, while her dancing partner Bill Robinson (Bojangles) shared accommodations with the black chauffeurs. Shirley may have been the first white actress allowed to hold hands with a black man in a feature film.

Every night, Gertrude coiled her daughter's hair into fifty-six pin-curls while her evening bedtime story was the next day's script. Accolade followed accolade: a miniature Oscar in 1935—the only one ever awarded to someone so young—her face appeared on a Wheaties box, her little handprints enshrined in the cement of Grauman's Chinese Theatre, a non-alcoholic drink christened after her. As the most popular star in Hollywood's firmament, with Clark Gable a distant second, her salary increased to $1,000 a week ($17,000 in today's currency); the biggest and littlest starlet declared her greatest wish was to own a pie factory when she grew up.

The hole in the Good Ship Lollipop appeared when Shirley grew less curly and more curvy, and audiences disliked the idea of their favorite baby blossoming into a babe. The fact that she was no longer a little girl was duly noted by *The Wizard of Oz* producer Arthur Freed, who offered her work at MGM, and at their first meeting, unzipped his pants. Naïve regarding male anatomy—shades of Wee Willie Winkie—Shirley giggled when she saw the unfamiliar male anatomy, and an infuriated Freed ordered her out of his office. Astute enough to realize America's love affair with Shirley was waning, Gertrude enrolled her in an exclusive girls' school, and the idea of being with her peers seemed more exciting than making a new movie.

At age seventeen, Shirley was a strong-willed chain-smoker and accepted a ring from a twenty-two-year-old Army Air Corps sergeant, John Agar, Jr. The intimate wedding she planned turned into a frenzy when twelve thousand uninvited guests mobbed her bridesmaids, ripping their blue organza dresses to tatters for souvenirs. Shirley was happy to trade

Hollywood for housewife, but Agar proved unequal to the task of the husband of a national institution, and his drinking and affairs led to divorce. Although their relationship had turned into a nightmare, Shirley said it brought her "something beautiful," her daughter, Linda Susan. Four months later, on a trip to Hawaii with her family, Shirley met wealthy businessman Charles Black, who claimed he had never seen a Shirley Temple movie. After her horrific marriage, she contacted her old friend J. Edgar Hoover to arrange an FBI background check. Charles and Shirley tied the knot after a brief courtship and raised Linda Susan and the two children they had together, Charles Jr., and Lori, in Woodside, California. They remained committed to one another until his passing after fifty-five years of marriage; the devastated widow never removed her late husband's voice from their answering machine.

Shirley felt a need to make another mark and traded in her childhood aspiration to own a pie factory for a career in politics. Her interest in international work came after doctors diagnosed her brother George with multiple sclerosis in 1952. She became active in local and international MS societies and helped found the federation of MS groups. Shirley hoped to emulate the Californian political success of her former costar Ronald Reagan, who had become governor. She did not garner enough votes; it did not help her chances that bands kept playing "On the Good Ship Lollipop" at campaign stops. In 1969, President Nixon appointed her to the five-member United States delegation to the United Nations General Assembly. She handled her position as professionally as she had her previous acting jobs, and spoke out about the problems of the aged, the plight of refugees, and environmental issues.

To Shirley's great chagrin, her childhood role as America's sweetheart continued to hurt her credibility. During her first ambassadorship appointment, Secretary of State Henry Kissinger heard her discussing Namibia at a party and "was surprised that I even knew the word." She had to prove herself over and over during an era when few women, let alone a pretty former actress, attained such a post. She persevered, and at age forty-one, President Nixon (in appreciation of her raising $2 million for his campaign) appointed her as a delegate to the United Nations. On an official trip to the Soviet Union in 1972, Shirley felt a burning sensation in her breast that led to a cancer diagnosis. She underwent a modified radical mastectomy and held a news conference in her hospital room to discuss her condition, years before Betty Ford had the courage to make the same announcement. Two years later, President Gerald Ford made her the Ambassador to the Republic of Ghana, where the one-time highest-paid movie star had to boil her drinking water, yet still declared her position "the best job I ever had." On one occasion, she dressed in a Ghanaian outfit of a printed cotton head scarf and gown, learned basic words in their language, and reached out to its working women, who she called her sisters. In 1976, she returned to Washington, and President Gerald Ford made her the first woman Chief of Protocol at the White House.

In her sixties, no one would have cast aspersion if—after working since childhood, an abusive first marriage, breast cancer, and the struggle to help her daughter, Lori, beat her heroin addiction—Temple had thought it time to put up the feet that had tap danced into the world's heart, but retirement held no appeal. She returned to diplomacy under President George H. W. Bush when, as the Iron Curtain was descending, she served as the ambassador to Czechoslovakia. Temple recalled, "I was told I was going to a Stalinist backwater, one of the toughest countries around. And I thought, "Good! Let's go get 'em!" When she arrived in Prague, she discovered that there had been a Shirley Temple fan club there fifty years earlier. Officials brought "Shirleyka," old membership cards, for her to autograph. Mrs. Temple Black succeeded beyond expectations, winning praise from Henry Kissinger who called her "very intelligent, very tough-minded, very disciplined." His words were an apt tribute to a woman who had left the silver screen saying she had "had enough of pretend."

Temple-Black also forged some unlikely alliances, such as the one with farm labor leader Cesar Chavez, who initially was reluctant to work with an ardent Republican. The two met for lunch and found they shared common interests in gardening and vegetarianism, as well as the value of union membership. The Clinton years ended her diplomatic career, but she remained active in groups such as the American Academy of Diplomacy.

In 2006, the Academy of Motion Pictures presented Shirley with a full-sized Oscar, having bestowed a miniature one fifty years before, and she dedicated it to her late mother. She did not expect much attention, as she had been long absent from the spotlight of Tinseltown, but her first clue that this was not the case came when Marisa Tomei gazed at her in rapture—and not because of her Oleg Cassini suit. Freshly Oscar-laden Helen Hunt and Robin Williams fussed over her, and the Academy's website lit up with more questions about Shirley than any other star. Black stated, "I've been so blessed. If someone asked me whom I would choose to be if I could come back in another life, I would have to say Shirley Temple Black."

At age eighty-five, Shirley Temple Black passed away at her Woodside home. If her death were a scene from a Hollywood film at its closing, she would have taken Mr. Bojangles's hand and together they would have tap-danced up the stairs.

CHAPTER EIGHTEEN

An Extraordinary Woman (1929)

Recipients of a genetic lottery—the "It Girls" of the runways—define the fashion industry. In the 1960s, Twiggy's skeletal frame launched the woman-waif; in the 1970s, gap-toothed Lauren Hutton illustrated imperfect perfection; in the 1990s, Gisele Bündchen's athletic build ended the era of heroin chic. But predating these ladies of the catwalk was one who defied the litmus test of beauty and proved it need not come with an expiration date.

The title of Anita Loo's book, *Gentlemen Prefer Blondes*, can serve as a metaphor for the history of the Western world. British missionaries camouflaged imperialism under the guise of "the white man's burden"; Nazi ideology apotheosized the Aryan ideal; Barbie glorified the blonde bombshell. Given this entrenched mindset, it is not surprising that the goddesses of the silver screen sported golden locks: Mary Pickford, Jean Harlow, Marilyn Monroe. Because of this cookie-cutter yardstick of aesthetics, those with darker pigment often harbored self-doubt, as was the case with a girl from the Far East who considered herself the proverbial ugly duckling.

Noelie (so called because of her arrival on Christmas Day, 1929) Dasouza Machado was born in Shanghai, the daughter of a Chinese mother (who passed away when she was three) and Frederico, a Portuguese father, a gold trader. She grew up in the city's tony enclave and spoke French in school, Portuguese at home, and Chinese with the servants. The Machados were pillars of their community, and the money fueling their wealth came courtesy of a boat-captain grandfather who shipped cotton and—considering their vast wealth—opium as well. Growing up with two brothers and a stepbrother, she never considered herself attractive. White, Western women—Irene Dunne, Vivien Leigh, Rita Hayworth, and Noelie's idol, Ava Gardner—beckoned from posters in Shanghai. She later recalled, "We (nonwhites) had no images. We had nothing that told us we were nice-looking, nothing. So, I didn't think of myself as good-looking at all." At age six, Noelie barely survived a combination of typhoid and meningitis, and endured a stay in quarantine, where she lay in a state of delirium. When Japanese bombs fell on her hospital, amidst the ensuing chaos, rescue crews mistook her for a corpse. Her father found her on a lorry, surrounded by the dead. The Japanese confiscated Frederico's business, as well as his palatial home, forcing him to move into a cramped apartment with his family and various relatives. When Noelie was sixteen, the Machados fled the newly Mao-controlled country; Frederico felt his mixed-heritage children would not mesh well with the new regime. As he put it, "We are neither fish nor fowl." They sailed to Buenos Aires where, because of her slanted eyes, the neighborhood children teased her with the name Chinita (little China girl.) Chinita was also what Buenos Aires's Lotharios called her as the teen made her way to the nuns at the Convent of the Sacred Heart. After graduation, she became a Pan American air hostess and lived with her brother in Lima, Peru.

"I'm coming to get you." These five words uttered over the telephone redirected the course of Noelie's life. The magnetic voice belonged to Luis Miguel Dominguin, the most famous bull-fighter in the world. Noelie reminisced, "I was swept away. Of course, he swept away ten million women, also." Luis was a fabled matador and Picasso pal, the kind of man other men wanted to be, and their wives wanted to be with. Their relationship exposed her to the world of the bullfight, one worthy of a Hemingway novel. Indeed, Hemingway chronicled Dominguin's fierce rivalry with his brother-in-law in a *Life* magazine series, later published as *The Dangerous*

Summer. Luis was immediately smitten by the teenager with the Oriental look, and three days later, they were living together. Their unwedded bliss scandalized Noelie's proper Roman Catholic family, including her oppressive stepmother, and it took fifteen years for her father to again speak to his only daughter. The fallout from their affair—Machado later said it was as if she had run away with Mick Jagger—forced them to escape the eye of the storm. The couple fled South America and embarked on city-hopping of the world's most glittering capitals. Luis' star status brought them into the orbit of celebrity parties where they fraternized with Errol Flynn ("a punk"), Pablo Picasso ("charming, flirtatious, old"), Charles Revson, owner of Revlon ("charming"), and Francois Truffaut. Their two-year tryst ended at a soiree in Madrid when Dominguin waved his "red flag" at Ava Gardner, then the wife of Frank Sinatra. Machado recalled, "Can you imagine the most beautiful woman in the world coming in and going after your guy? I had no chance." Devastated at the breakup and estranged from her parents, Machado made her way to Paris, never dreaming it would lead to her road less travelled.

The exquisite, exotic DNA that had forced the Machados to escape China proved a siren call to the head honchos of the top fashion houses, who were intrigued with Noelie's sky-high cheekbones, frame made for designer clothes, and luxuriant black hair. She was soon the highest paid freelance runway model in Europe, and became for future generations the non-white beauty icon she had never had for herself. Noelie sashayed down the runways, a Madame Butterfly in Balenciaga. Along the way, she decided her very Catholic name did little to enhance her unusual looks and her burgeoning career on the haute circuit. In a nod to her country of birth and the racial slur of her youth, she adopted the moniker China (pronounced Cheena.) Paris led not only to fame but also to Martin La Salle, the son of a diplomat and political science student at the Sorbonne. She recalled, "He was extraordinarily handsome, a mixture of Henry Fonda and Montgomery Clift—simply gorgeous." Despite his looks, for a year during their courtship, she left him for the Oscar-winning actor William Holden. La Salle and China married soon after their reconciliation, and the couple had two daughters, Blanche and Emmanuelle. Divorce arrived in 1965 when China had an affair with her husband's friend, a New York-based writer for *Paris Match.*

The furor over the model who broke the mold reached Oleg Cassini, who brought her to New York for his 1958 show. When Cassini contacted a group of Southern buyers to inquire why they had not placed any orders for the dresses Ms. Machado had worn, their succinct response was, "Oh, she's black." Nevertheless, her American debut led to the door of the grande dame of fashion, Diana Vreeland, who championed Machado's unusual aesthetic. The night they met, Vreeland threw Machado into a show at the Waldorf Astoria, which Noelie opened atop a twenty-foot ladder in bat-winged Balenciaga hot pink pajamas. *Harper's Bazaar's* crown prince photographer, Richard Avedon, watched with admiration as she descended, and booked her on the spot. He pronounced China his muse, referring to her as "Golden Bones," and dubbed her "the most beautiful woman in the world." Avedon photographed her in various locales, such as on an ice floe in Canada, wrapped in snow leopard, shots that garnered global attention. The erotic and ethnic-faced model presented an image that Hearst's white-bread readers could not put their manicured fingers on, much less identify with. A furor arose when Avedon wanted his pictures of Ms. Machado in the pages of the February issue; however, the publisher refused: "Listen, we can't publish these pictures. The girl is not white." As his contract with *Harper's Bazaar* was up for renewal, he threatened to leave if his work with China was not included. Such was Avedon's clout that the editors concurred. Machado, in addition to serving as the magazine's first nude, was the first non-Caucasian woman to grace the cover of an American magazine. Through becoming the Jackie Robinson of fashion, China set the stage for a representation of beauty considerably more inclusive than the blonde-haired, blue-eyed standard of the 1960s, and paved the way for Beverly Johnson, Iman, and Naomi Campbell.

In 1962, China segued from her role in front of the camera to one behind it when she became the fashion director of *Harper's Bazaar*, thus opening up another professional pathway, this time for women. Some of her famed subjects, Elizabeth Taylor and Judy Garland, aided in her endeavor by lifelong friend Avedon. A decade later, she branched out to produce fashion shows for television, design costumes for films, and launch a namesake line of wraps. She also helped introduce *Lear's*, a magazine aimed at "the woman who wasn't born yesterday"—heady accomplishments for a single mother. In her free time, she spent evenings partying with Andy Warhol at Studio 54 and hung out with celebrities such as Jack Nicholson.

Even in China's eighties, maturity never looked so good. She did not kick off her designer heels and rest after a storied life—one that took her from China to Latin America to Europe to the States—and retire in her golden years. And golden they were. Firm in her refusal to live off the fruits of a man, Machado made a comfortable living from her varied enterprises and savvy real estate investments that allowed her to purchase a white waterfront property on the spectacular Long Island Sound, in the exclusive enclave of the Hamptons. She shared her multi-million-dollar home with her second husband, Ricardo Rosa, and their dog Cha Cha, a French bulldog with a penchant for chewing on telephone cords. But the chic eccentric Asian-themed '50s house was no Sunset Boulevard. Machado, forever in constant motion, painted the living room murals shortly after the death of Avedon as a way of mitigating her grief. Until her eighth decade, China was the hostess of an annual June party to celebrate the blooming of her roses. An accomplished chef, she cooked everything for her 110 guests using Macao recipes, compliments of her father, a mixture of the cuisines of China, Portugal, and India. Never one to rest on her laurels, in addition to an autobiography, *I Was Always Running After the Laughter,* China worked on a cookbook about the cuisine of her childhood, and globe-trotted to exotic locales such as India.

Machado returned to her old stomping ground despite her protestations of, "I'm a senior citizen, for God's sake!" when she signed a modeling contract at the age of eighty. Thus, the woman who broke the color barrier shattered the age one as well. She appeared in a twenty-page spread in *W* magazine, and it brought in such an avalanche of offers that she described it as "complete madness." At age eighty-two, she was featured in advertising for the New York store, Barney's, and landed a spot in Cole Haan's "Born in 1928" campaign, to celebrate the brand's and her own eighty-fifth birthday, alongside other octogenarians such as Maya Angelou. Ivan Bart, the president of IMG Models, said, "China was instrumental in teaching younger models with her advice, "Own yourself, own your own beauty.'" Her life showed them how.

In 2011, a reporter went to the Machado home for a lunch date, and China provided the directions: "Drive straight to the end of the road. We're on the beach. You can come right in. I am an ordinary person." However, after the interview— where his subject was decked out in head-to-toe faded denim Levis—was proof positive that ordinary was the last word to describe an extraordinary woman.

CHAPTER NINETEEN

Lead Once More (1929)

A spurious story recounts that President Lincoln told Harriet Beecher Stowe, author of *Uncle Tom's Cabin*, "So you're the little woman who started this great war." A century later, another little woman ignited another civil war, though the warring flags were neither Union nor Confederate. Instead, the banner bore the colors of the biblical Joseph's coat.

One never knows on whom the spotlight of fame will land, as was the case with Edith (Edie), born in Philadelphia, the youngest of three children of James and Cecelia Schlain, Jewish immigrants from Russia. The family lost their candy/ice cream store and home above it after Edie and a brother contracted polio and the authorities quarantined the shop. James sheltered Edie as best he could during the Depression: he took a hard-boiled-egg sandwich for lunch to work at his new job, so he could buy her books. Her mother's advice concerning anti-Semitism was that, if a boy called her "dirty Jew," she should pull his hair and run. The family moved to a middle-class neighborhood because Mrs. Schlain wanted her daughters to meet the right boys.

In 1946, Edie attended Temple University and got engaged to her brother's best friend, Saul Windsor, whom she married after she received her bachelor's degree. She later recalled, "He was exactly what most girls wanted. He was big, handsome, and strong, yet sweet. I think that if I had been straight, he would have been the love of my life." She had feared that she was not, even before walking down the aisle. Less than a year later, she divorced Saul because she wanted something else from love, something that required remarkable chutzpah in

1952. Edie moved to Greenwich Village to "let myself be gay,"
and she pursued a master's degree in mathematics at New
York University. She applied for a job programming the eight-
ton UNIVAC computer that required high-security clearance.
Windsor found her niche at IBM, where she attained the
company's highest technical ranking, an extremely rare feat
for a woman of that era. She felt it advisable to keep her love
of ladies secret from her employer and colleagues and was in
constant fear of being outed.

Her life's most magical moment occurred when she went
to Portofino in Greenwich Village, when she discovered that
on Friday nights, it was full of lesbians, and she was desperate
to meet someone. Two years younger than Edie, Thea Spyer
was a stunning psychology student, an accomplished violinist,
and had the dubious distinction of having been expelled by
Sarah Lawrence College for kissing a woman. She had been
born in Amsterdam to a wealthy Jewish family of pickle
manufacturers whose fortune allowed them to flee Holland
just before the Nazis invaded. Although Spyer arrived with
another woman, she and Edie danced until, as Windsor put
it, she got a hole in her stocking. Edie said she "had never
wanted anybody inside me till Thea. And then I wanted her
inside me all the time." They saw each other at parties over
the next two years, and during those meetings, they would
dance together. Thea recalled that Edie was the "first lesbian
I ever met who could actually lead!" Thea, for her part, was
taken by Edie's physical allure: platinum blonde hair—Clairol
No. 103—trim figure, and ample cleavage. Windsor admitted,
"If I didn't have nice breasts, Thea and I would never have
got together." Nevertheless, Spyer, highly sought after, wanted
to play the field, though Edie had been instantly smitten.
In 1965, Windsor went to the Hamptons knowing her love
interest would be there. When they met, Edie asked her if her
dance card was full, to which Thea replied, "It is now." Edie
remembered, "We made love all afternoon and went dancing
at night—and that was the beginning." To explain why Thea
often called her at work, she invented a relationship with

Spyer's "brother Willy," actually the name of her childhood doll. Their family dynamics were also problematic. Spyer's relatives in New York disapproved of their relationship, so the couple spent the first few Thanksgivings after they became engaged at Edie's sister's house in Philadelphia. That ended because her brother-in-law was not keen on spending time with his sister and her lesbian lover.

The ladies loved to travel, and their first trip was to Suriname; Spyer chose the destination, as it was Dutch-speaking, and she wanted to impress Windsor by conversing with the locals. They traipsed all over Europe with half a dozen enormous coordinating suitcases. On a trip to St. Thomas, just after they had moved in together in a Greenwich Village home, Windsor said, "I bought all the stuff I thought you need for a nice Jewish home." Unfortunately, that home could not include the children for whom Edie longed. Parenthood was not in the cards: Dr. Spyer was a psychologist working in a field that classified her sexual orientation as a mental illness. Marriage was the impossible dream as well, but in 1967, Spyer knelt down and proposed. Instead of an engagement ring that would have raised questions about her hubby-to-be, Thea gave Edie a brooch, a circle of diamonds.

In 1977, when Spyer was forty-five, she received a diagnosis of chronic progressive multiple sclerosis. The couple still indulged in their beloved pastime, with Thea ditching her crutches on the dance floor and leading with her good leg. The dire disease was also powerless to end their wanderlust. In Windsor's bedroom, she placed a photograph of Thea being helped up a hill in Jerusalem by female Israeli soldiers. In the documentary *Edie and Thea: A Very Long Engagement,* Sayer reported, "Here I am, quadriplegic, not much is moving. The only thing that'll bring me to tears—the only thing—is dancing. When we're at parties or anything, anybody asks Edie to dance, she doesn't do it." Despite the affliction, their sex life was never on the back burner. Edie retired from IBM to serve as her lover's caregiver and never approved when people regarded her as a lesbian Florence Nightingale. "I was never her nurse—I'm her lover! I was just doing things to make her comfortable—and that was with loving her and *digging* her. I don't know if I'd glorify it."

After their forty-year engagement, and with the Grim Reaper beckoning, Edie and Thea—ages seventy-seven and seventy-five—legalized their union; Windsor was no longer content with the idea of merely "pulling his hair and running"—her mother's old mantra. The brides, along with six friends, flew to Toronto—an excruciating feat for a quadriplegic—where the ceremony was officiated by Canada's first openly gay judge, Justice Harvey Brownstone. Less than two years later, Spyer passed away.

To add to the sorrow of the then-octogenarian widow, the IRS levied a $363,000 federal tax on her late wife's estate, something it would not have done if Thea had been Theo. Edie was almost eighty, suffering from a broken heart, and within a few weeks, suffered a heart attack to add to the mix. When she recovered, she decided to take her country to court, though she realized it was akin to fighting City Hall. Approaching her ninth decade, Edie embarked on a judicial odyssey, fighting a battle she had never expected to wage, and in the process, she became an accidental activist. A number of attorneys refused to take her case, as they worried she was too old, and might die along the way. She eventually found a champion in Roberta Kaplan, who took the suit pro bono with the provision that Windsor was not to talk publicly about sex, a subject about which Edie was less than close-mouthed.

Kaplan successfully argued the case in front of the Supreme Court, and on that 2013 red-letter day, a photograph captured Windsor marching out of the Capitol, a woman in her eighties, wearing a bright pink scarf, smiling. The picture spoke the proverbial thousand words: that, after all the years of rejection from family members, employers, and the government, members of the LGBT community no longer had to hide. Indeed, in case anyone was in doubt as to Windsor's sexual orientation, she wore a t-shirt which proclaimed, "Nobody knows I'm a lesbian." Although Queen Elizabeth and Edie shared the surname of Windsor, the commonality ends there.

After the 5-4 Supreme Court ruling in *Windsor v. the United States,* the eighty-four-year-old plaintiff was at Roberta's apartment with a group of friends when she received a congratulatory call from President Obama. Windsor said of the historic moment, "If I had to survive Thea, what a glorious way to do it." While the others cried and yelled, Edie announced, "I want to go to Stonewall right now." To celebrate, Roberta and Edie took a victory lap around Manhattan in an SUV, their version of the Popemobile; every time they stopped, fans swarmed the car, weeping tears of joy, and in return received a kiss from the matriarch of their movement. She said, "If you have to outlive a great love, I can't think of a better way to do it than being everyone's hero."

Ms. Windsor's activism continued after her victory, and during the summer of 2017, she maintained a pace that would have been impressive for someone half her age. She was a fixture at marches and events for homeless LGBT youth, lesbian rights, and violence against gays. The eighty-four-year-old became the Rosa Parks of same-sex marriage activists. She drove a convertible, albeit with disregard for stop signs, and she made plans to go on a Caribbean cruise with Maya Angelou. The diminutive woman was the Grand Marshal of the New York City Pride Parade and a runner-up, alongside Pope Francis, for *Time* magazine's Person of the Year.

Ariel Levy wrote in the *New Yorker* that, in 2015, she went to visit the grande dame of gay rights in Provincetown, Massachusetts. Windsor enjoyed celebrity status in the community, and as they walked down Commercial Street, past the rainbow flags and the stores selling leather harnesses and lobster t-shirts, strangers approached and embraced the tiny octogenarian to thank her for her bravery that had paved the way for a more perfect union. Her friend was as glamorous as ever that summer, with her platinum bob and huge black sunglasses, effervescent even in the midst of a breakup. The problem with the relationship, she explained, was that the woman—thirty years her junior—simply could not keep up with her sexual needs. Windsor said, "I told her, Honey, I'm not demanding—I'm begging!" Levy said that, around midnight, she told Windsor that she should probably bike back to her room, so Edie could get some sleep. The response from the woman who always advised not to postpone joy: "Sleep! Are you kidding, cookie? I want to go dancing!" The comment would not have surprised anyone who knew Edie; after all, she was not your typical Jewish old lady.

In 2016, Windsor took her third trip down the aisle when she wed Judith Kasen, then fifty-one, no doubt someone who could keep up with her. Rather than rue the reversal in the law that came too late for Thea, she stated, "The truth is, I never expected less from my country."

The white-haired heroine, not a stranger to swearing, partial to pearls, who favored running shoes—a fitting choice for a woman who never seemed to stop moving—passed away in 2017. And if Heaven is more forgiving than the land below, Thea will lead once more.

CHAPTER TWENTY

Viva La Causa (1930)

Ironically, the World War II poster of Rosie the Riveter, with its caption, "We can do it!" was the brainchild of a man, though it became a symbol of female empowerment. In contrast, the slogan of the United Farm Workers, attributed to Cesar Chavez, was authored by a woman—one whom history regulated to a footnote due to an amalgam of sexism and ageism.

Juliet, on her Verona balcony, concluded that one's name held no significance, yet this belief did not hold true for a baby born in the mining town of Dawson, New Mexico. Her parents, Juan and Alicia Fernandez, christened her Dolores (Spanish for sorrow), and her eighty-plus years have brought more than her fair share of heartache. She described her father as charismatic, intelligent, handsome, and chauvinistic, the latter of which contributed to the couple's divorce when Dolores was three. Alicia took her children to Stockton, California, where she refused to follow the machismo way, and raised her two sons and daughter as equals.

As a teenager, Dolores' passion was dance, and she received free lessons under the Works Progress Administration. Her aspiration was to one day become a professional dancer. This goal ended when her father, a former coal miner, became a union leader and a member of the New Mexico state legislature, piquing her interest in California's exploited laborers. Her empathy had also been honed by the neighborhood immigrants, who toiled under extreme heat for little pay and even less respect. Dolores determined that the best way she could serve her community was through education; she enrolled in the local University of the Pacific's Delta College teaching program.

At age twenty, she married Ralph Head, a manual laborer, with whom she had two daughters. In the classroom, she was appalled when students came to school hungry and barefoot, and determined she could make more of a difference as an advocate for reform. Her commitment to the cause increased after she witnessed police brutality against workers agitating for better wages. At age twenty-five, she joined the Stockton Community Organization, a local group that lobbied for Mexican-Americans through political and civic engagement. Aided by her innate gift of oratory, and refusing to acknowledge the word no, Dolores became a voice for the voiceless. She founded the Agricultural Workers Association to protect the marginalized against the powerful, and ruthless, grape growers' interests. Despite her grueling schedule, she tried her luck at a second marriage with Ventura Huerta, and the four children of their union joined her two daughters from her first marriage. An insight into Dolores as a young woman is apparent when a female reporter asked her what she would do if someone gave her $5,000 to spend on herself. She responded that she would donate it to the movement. When the journalist persisted and asked if she did not have the average woman's dream of pampering herself, Dolores answered, "To me, being at a spa and having a new hairdo would be a terrible waste of time."

Dolores' Marx-meets-Engels moment came with her introduction to Cesar Chavez; their common vision was galvanizing the oppressed. In 1962, they launched the National Farm Workers Association, a precursor to the later United Farm Workers. Three years later, Dolores was a lead organizer for one of the most famous protests in US history, which lasted more than five years: the Table Grape Boycott. They knew they could not succeed on their own, and enlisted the conscience of the nation; seventeen million Americans refused to eat grapes or lettuce, or drink Gallo wine. The little lady (she was five foot two) faced off against powerful foes: the politically connected landowners (who called her the dragon lady), California's Republican governor

Ronald Reagan, and President Richard Nixon. And yet David triumphed over Goliath. Their efforts bore fruit and resulted in the first contract between farm workers, growers, and the establishment of the United Farm Workers Labor Union. This victory was staggering; at the time, this labor force— poor, and in many cases undocumented—were considered impossible to mobilize. They were subjected to horrific working conditions: wages as low as ninety cents an hour, and without toilets, cold drinking water, breaks, or protection from pesticides. Although the thirty-six-year-old Dolores, rather than Cesar, had been the architect of the victory and the one who had exhorted women to join the struggle, these facts were expunged from the historical record. In all the iconic photographs, the workers are holding up the contract along with Chavez and the other male power players. Similarly, Cesar was given credit as the originator of Dolores' iconic slogan, "*Si se puede.*" When Barack Obama used the slogan as a political rallying cry, Huerta's name never came up. The former president righted the wrong in 2012, when he awarded the leader the Medal of Freedom and joked, "Dolores was very gracious when I told her I had stolen her slogan." Although Chavez passed away in 1993, he still eclipses Huerta as the one who launched the movement, and there are countless monuments, street signs, and a holiday dedicated to the hero of the workers. Angela Davis explains this historical white-washing, "The assumption was that Chavez was the leader, and she was the housekeeper." Because of her sex, and because she was sixty-three, the union refused to pass her the baton of leadership, although she had been its co-founder.

At the time, Huerta did not question this sin of omission; as a child of the pre-women's-lib era, despite her liberal upbringing, she still bought into the supremacy of the patriarchy. This mindset was altered in the late 1960s, when she went to New York and worked with Gloria Steinem for the nationwide grape boycott and met other powerhouse women, such as Angela Davis. When she returned to California, she was no longer willing to buy into the time-honored protocol of male supremacy and was determined to take credit for her accomplishments. Dolores also left an impression on Ms. Steinem, who said, "I know she set me on fire about racial injustice. I would not be able to see what's hidden in the fields of our country without Dolores." Awakened to gender inequality, Dolores later referred to herself as a born-again feminist when she revised her views on abortion. As a Catholic, she had always eschewed the procedure; however, after her exposure to Women's Liberation, she felt it a constitutional right to have control over one's body, free from governmental control. She felt the pro-choice movement was important for the Latina field laborers whose large number of offspring ensured lives of dire privation. "As Coretta Scott King said, we won't ever have peace in the world until women take power. And when I say the word women, I may as well use the word feminist. Not all women are feminists, but feminists are people that care about immigrants and workers and the environment and labor rights, and of course reproductive rights, LGBT rights."

When Dolores' second marriage collapsed, she began a relationship with Richard Chavez, Cesar's younger brother, and the couple decided the best way to help the workers was to live among them. Her opponents, including the Teamsters, tried to shame her for having eleven children with three different men—four out of wedlock—and for the fact that she was not at home looking after them. These allegations proved hurtful, as Dolores was always confronted with her own version of Sophie's Choice: spending time with her family, or fighting for her cause. When interviewed, her children recalled with a mixture of pride and pain the sacrifices they were forced to make, as Dolores was often the mother of thousands rather than one to them. Her daughter said she was always "off and running"; a son revealed that it took ten months for her to realize that he had dropped out of high school. Another ruefully said, "The movement became her most important child. There are scars because of that." Dolores explained the reason behind her activism: "It was such a calling. I felt it so strongly. This is the reason I live."

Unfortunately, like old habits, prejudice is hard to shake. In 1988, presidential candidate George H. W. Bush was speaking at a fundraiser at San Francisco's St. Francis Hotel. For the firebrand activist, then fifty-eight, it was just another day at "the office"; she was handing out leaflets on the UFW's long-standing grape boycott, something she had done on countless occasions. However, this time, the police moved in. A baton struck the diminutive protestor, shattering her ribs and rupturing her spleen. Her injuries required emergency surgery, and she was hospitalized for a month. The assault was captured on video, and her lawsuit resulted in a significant settlement and police department reforms. It did not, however, end her mission. In a speech, she made her plea: "Sisters, brothers, feminists, all of us, we have got a lot of hard work to do. When Dr. King was at that great march in Washington, he said to the people at that great march, 'Go back to Alabama. Go back to Mississippi. Go back and organize.' This is the message I want to say to all of my sisters and brothers. We've got to organize."

Until 2017, Ms. Huerta was one of the most important freedom fighters most people had never heard of. This situation changed with the release of the documentary *Dolores* that aimed to put her where she belongs—alongside Malcolm X, Dr. King, Cesar Chavez, and Gloria Steinem—as one of the most important of American agitators for reform. The film debuted the night before women across the world marched for equality and human rights. Dolores was at the protest; after all, where else would she be? In Park City, Utah, she spoke at a rally following a march organized by Chelsea Handler, where she led a chant of "*Si se puede.*" For many in the crowd, this rally was their first public demonstration; Dolores had been doing it for seven decades.

The documentary was the brainchild of guitar god Carlos Santana, who served as executive producer. His mother, Josephina Barragan de Santana, had been insistent that her son shine a long-overdue spotlight on the eighty-eight-year-old activist who had given her blood, sweat, and tears to better the lives of the marginalized. When he heard the story of Dolores, he called her the real-life Wonder Woman. He added, "I would like to see Dolores Huerta parks, libraries, freeways, schools. I would like her to have her own TV channel, running twenty-four hours a day." It was a soft sell to get the producer Peter Bratt, brother of the actor Benjamin Bratt, on board, as the director was the son of a Peruvian-born mother who had marched with Dolores. Fortunately, a wealth of archival material showed her in action in the trenches throughout six and a half decades. Bratt refers to Dolores as the Forrest Gump of activism because of her connection to some of the great movers and movements of her era: in 1968 Robert F. Kennedy honored her moments before his assassination at the Ambassador Hotel, and she was a participant in Black Lives Matter and Standing Rock protests. Cesar Chavez used to say, "The only time you lose is when you quit," and, though Dolores is approaching her ninth decade, quitting is something she does not intend to do. She must remain up and running as long as injustice remains.

As a girl, Dolores had wanted to be a dancer, and in her fashion, she has achieved that goal. She has made activism an art form. Her remarkable life can be encapsulated in the words of a poster she once stood in front of, "*Viva La Causa.*"

CHAPTER TWENTY-ONE

Said Sister Megan Never (1930)

When Henry David Thoreau, jailed for nonpayment of taxes as a protest against slavery, received a visit from Ralph Waldo Emerson, the latter asked, "David, what are you doing in there?" Thoreau replied, "Ralph, what are you doing out there?" A contemporary Thoreau is an octogenarian nun, her place of activism not Walden Pond, but Oak Ridge, Tennessee.

Megan Gillespie Rice, the woman born to be the poster child of protest, was the youngest of three girls raised in Manhattan, a block away from Barnard College. Her father, Dr. Frederick Rice, was a professor of obstetrics and routinely treated indigent women at Bellevue Hospital. Her mother, Madeleine Newman Hooke Rice, held a doctorate from Columbia University and taught history at Hunter College. Megan said her mother was strongly in favor of interracial marriage—a radical view in her era—and told her daughters, "I just can't wait until everybody in the world is tan!"

Megan was fifteen when the headlines read, "*A-Bomb Dropped on Hiroshima.*" Her uncle was in Nagasaki and witnessed its devastation. Rice said she had been aware since age nine of a government program so secretive that the European scientist who lived next door could not talk about his work, even to his spouse. Discussions about politics, the war, and its resultant refugee crisis of the 1940s were frequent at the dinner table. Her parents were staunch supporters of Dorothy Day and her Catholic Worker Movement and championed her throughout the Great Depression. Megan attended religious schools, and at age eighteen, she found her calling as a nun in the Order of the Catholic Society of the

Holy Child Jesus. She earned a bachelor's degree at Fordham and a master's in biology at Boston College. In 1962, upon graduation, she traded New York for Nigeria. Sister Megan helped build the school where she later taught, slept in a classroom while it was under construction, and lived in a rural village without electricity or running water. And there she remained for thirty years.

In the late 1980s, Megan returned to the States when malaria and typhoid fever impeded her work; remembering her uncle's graphic images of the destruction wrought by the nuclear bomb, ever the '60s hippie, she and other peace activists knelt in the Nevada test site to block a government truck. The police took her—along with her eighty-four-year-old mother—into custody. It would be the first of forty to fifty times she would find herself behind bars. Had the Sister worn a habit, she would have exchanged it for striped garb. In 1998, she took another ride in a paddy wagon when she protested at the Army's School of the Americas in Fort Benning, Georgia. Her anger stemmed from her belief that it taught generations of Latin American soldiers to fight leftist insurgencies, and many graduates participated in human rights abuses in their home countries. Sister Rice, who served six months in federal prison, said of her stay, "It was a great eye-opener. When you've had a prison experience, it minimizes your needs very much." And, regarding Sister Megan, to borrow the phrase from Al Jolson, "You ain't seen nothing yet, folks."

In the 1960s, Sally Field was the flying nun; in 2012, Megan Rice became the nuclear nun. Armed with flashlights, bolt cutters, and blood held in baby bottles, the eighty-two-year-old Sister and two accomplices—a carpenter and a Vietnam War veteran, members of the Transform Now Plowshares Movement—made their way to the Y-12 National Security Complex, a nuclear weapons plant referred to as the Fort Knox of Uranium, in Oak Ridge, Tennessee. The route, undertaken in the cover of night, was daunting for a woman in her eighties who had a mild heart condition.

Their plan involved walking through a wooded area for two hours, crawling underneath four fences, and eluding guards authorized to use lethal force. Sister Megan never wavered, as she felt the Holy Spirit was their guide. Upon arrival, they cut the last of the barbed wire and draped a banner on it with a drawing of a nuclear weapon and the words, "Never Again." Afterward, they proceeded to splatter human blood on the $548-million facility, encircled by enormous towers, and spray-painted anti-war slogans. One of these was a passage from the Book of Isaiah, "They will beat their swords into plowshares, and their spears into pruning hooks; nation shall not lift up sword against nation, neither shall they learn war anymore." Against the concrete fortification, they laid bibles and white roses, the latter an allusion to the White Rose, a German student group that had opposed Hitler, a move that led to their beheadings. As an added touch, they affixed yellow crime-scene tape to the building of mass destruction. Around 4:30 in the morning, a patrol car appeared as they were singing a modified version of a Gospel song, "This little light of mine, let it shine all around Y-12." Kirk Garland, a guard, gazed in astonishment at the intruders, locked himself in his SUV and called for backup. The Three Musketeers of nuclear disarmament stood beside his car door, said God had sent them, offered him some bread, and read a statement. It began, "Today, through our nonviolent Action, We, Transform Now Plowshares, indict the US Government nuclear modernization program." Garland warned them not to make any sudden movements or remove anything from their backpacks. The two men ignored him and reached into their bags, pulled out candles, lit them, and offered him one. When Sergeant Chad Riggs arrived, he drew his gun, ordered the three suspects to the ground, and handcuffed them. The Plowshares' action at Y-12 attracted international attention. The fact that three people, who were not trained Israeli commandos—let alone an octogenarian nun with a heart condition—could get up close and personal to the nation's stockpile of weapons left the government with considerable mud on its face.

The protestors offered an indictment accusing the United States of crimes against humanity and compared the morality of cutting the barbed wire at Y-12 to that of cutting those at Auschwitz. Federal prosecutors fired back with an indictment of their own. They charged Sister Rice and her two co-conspirators with trespassing on government property (a misdemeanor), as well as its destruction (a felony), that carried penalties of up to thirty years in prison and fines of up to $600,000. The Plowshares pleaded not guilty. They argued a nuclear plant was a threat to the planet, and the cost of maintaining the deadly enterprise would be better spent addressing socioeconomic woes. In her defense, Sister Megan stated that nuclear weapons, not the protest against them, posed the real threat to America's national security. Rice asked the judge for permission to let a short song be sung "to lighten the atmosphere," and he concurred. She turned to the gallery, overflowing with supporters, and together they raised their voices, "Sacred the land, sacred the water, sacred the sky, holy and true." The fact Rice was a silver-haired nun in her eighties played to the court of public opinion much more than had she been a twenty-something anti-nuke crusader; eleven thousand people signed a petition calling for her release. The prosecution argued that advanced age and religious affiliation should not be a mitigating factor. The jury found them guilty after little more than two hours, and Sister Megan's sentence entailed three years in the Metropolitan Detention Center in Brooklyn. Judge Thapar stated, "I know you want a life sentence and I just can't accommodate that request. Not only am I confident that you will live long past any sentence I give you, but I am sure that you will continue to use that brilliant mind you have. I only hope you'll use it to effectuate change in Washington rather than crimes in Tennessee." The defense team decided against an appeal, as the trio proclaimed they were guilty as charged and were proud of their actions.

The nun said she bonded with her fellow inmates, many of them drug addicts, victims of an economic system that invested in weapons rather than people. She railed against the horrible conditions where 100 women coexisted in one single, large bunk-bed filled room. The communal cell was the site of almost all daily activities, taking meals, exercising, and sleeping. There was never a moment of privacy, and the noise was "shrieking loud." To corroborate her account, the *New York Daily News* described the cramped living conditions as "a hellhole."

Lawyers, working pro bono, fought the charges, and two years later an appellate court ruled that the government had overreached in charging them with sabotage and the 85-year-old was set free. True to form, Sister Megan reacted to her release in a unique fashion, saying, "I felt it was an absolute grace to be there, among those people who are brave, suffering victims of the state. I was really sad when I had to leave." The government ordered the saboteurs to pay restitution, but since Rice had taken a vow of poverty decades ago, she had neither the intention nor the means.

Josh Harkinson, a journalist for *Mother Jones,* asked how she felt to be free; her response, "Not that much different, because none of us is free. And it looks like we are going to go on being unfree for as long as there's a nuclear weapon waiting." When questioned on *Democracy Now!* about her life as a nun in prison, Rice gave a response worthy of Sister Jane Ingalls, a character based on her, from *Orange is the New Black.* "They are the ones who are the wisest in this country," she said of her fellow inmates. "They know what is really happening. They are the fallout of nuclear weapons production."

The leftist rabble-rouser joyfully reconnected with family and friends and took time to visit St. Patrick's Cathedral. Still spry, despite her advanced age and her incarceration, she made her way on her own through the crowded streets of

Manhattan. Her first purchase: peanut butter frozen yogurt topped with hot fudge. Afterwards, she was back to business, and in her case, this entailed conferring with her superiors about her future—one in which she planned to continue her anti-nuclear activism. Asked if she was worried that further protests would land her once again behind bars, she replied, "It would be an honor. Good Lord, what would be better than to die in prison for the anti-nuclear cause?" She added that her faith was inextricably interwoven with her cause. "Our faith is the God of life. These weapons represent the very destruction of life." Despite all her hardships—a remote African village, numerous lock-down facilities—the 85-year-old said her life has been one of privilege, and she was grateful. No doubt she was referring to privilege, not in reference to a life of wealth or of leisure, but one in which she was the handmaiden of Jesus.

In an interview for the British newspaper the *Guardian*, she showed up wearing donated clothes: blue jeans and a denim shirt. When the journalist told her that jeans-on-jeans was a very fashionable look for the season, the compliment took her by surprise. After a moment, she responded, "Ah. You are saying that I am in fashion," and gifted him with a smile. "I care about the way I look," said Sister Megan never.

Said Sister Megan Never (1930)

CHAPTER TWENTY-TWO

The Jet (1931)

In 1982, cartoonist Bob Thaves said of Fred Astaire, "Sure he was great, but don't forget that Ginger Rogers did everything he did...backwards and in high heels." Another female dancer shared the same handicap as Ms. Rogers, with the additional burden of being Latina in a white world.

A sense of security is a basic human need, and this concept holds especially true for children. Security was torn from Rosa Dolores Alverio when she was five years old. In her memoir, she described the land of her birth as "the most sensual place in the world," near the Puerto Rican rainforest. Her mother (also named Rosa, who had her daughter at age seventeen) decided to forego natural beauty for a chance at material wealth, and, leaving her cheating husband (the first of five) and son Francisco behind, she and her daughter immigrated to the United States. Later, in a throaty Cheech and Chong accent, little Rosa recalled that, when they approached the Statue of Liberty, she thought "a lady runs dees country." Although that was not the case, a woman did run her life; she had the quintessential stage mother. New York was a forest of a different sort, cold and replete with racism. They ended up in a dismal shared apartment in the Bronx, a transition that Rosa compared to *The Wizard of Oz* in reverse (from warm, glorious color to inhospitable black and white). Unable to communicate in English, her form of expression was dance, and Mrs. Alverio's double shift as a seamstress paid for lessons from Paco Cansino, Rita Hayworth's uncle. Before she was ten, Rosa was performing what she calls a "Carmen Miranda act" at weddings, and she also dubbed Spanish voices for various actresses in movies.

Armed with beauty and talent, at age sixteen she dropped out of high school and headed for Hollywood. The first movie star she met was Clark Gable, who told her, "Rosita. Great name, kid." Bill Grady, a casting agent, disagreed and tried out alternatives: Ruby Fontino, Marcy Miranda, Orchid Montenegro. Then he hit on Rita, after Rita Hayworth; her surname Moreno was compliments of her stepfather. In an interview with Louis B. Mayer—one of the Ms in MGM Studios—at the Waldorf-Astoria, the famed director took one look at the sultry teen, who had made up her face to resemble Elizabeth Taylor, and seconds later said, "Sign her up!" Her voluptuous beauty caught the eye of many men, some old enough to be her father. One of these was a handsome, red-headed gentleman at a hotel, who sat next to a regal woman. Rita later wrote of this encounter, "His hairline moved back an inch, as when a predatory animal spots his prey and paralyzes it with 'that look.' It was obviously lust at first sight, and I remember thinking, 'Whooo, this guy don't waste no time!'" Weeks later, she saw her admirer in *Life* magazine—the young senator from Massachusetts, John F. Kennedy, with his wife, Jackie.

Men were always quite "friendly." In Rita's first movie, *So Young, So Bad* (1950), she played a suicidal teenager. The 1940s matinee idol Paul Henreid "used the scenes of cutting down my dead body as an excuse to run his hands over my breasts." Due to her ethnicity, whether she played Arabians, Polynesians, or Mexicans, her parts involved, "You tink you fool Lolita? Ha!" She was the "sexy spitfire" with a false accent; she had lost her own to meld into a New York City that had not yet experienced the great Puerto Rican migration.

Moreno's big break came when she landed a role in the twentieth-century version of *Romeo and Juliet, West Side Story*, where the fire escapes of Manhattan replaced Verona's balcony. Rita played the sexy, skirt-twirling girlfriend of a Puerto Rican gang leader and, as Anita, danced her way into America's heart. Moreno said, "Anita was the very first

Hispanic character I had ever played who had dignity, a sense of self-respect, and was loving. She became my role model." Although the production was mostly a labor of love, the scene where the rival gang members pinned Anita to the floor in Doc's candy store, taunted her with racial epithets, and threatened her with rape, left her an inconsolable blubbering wreck. The actors had called her the sorts of terrible names she had not heard since her Bronx childhood. Rita said of the encounter, "It was coming from my entrails. Sometimes old wounds don't heal." After her historic achievement of being the first Hispanic to win an Academy Award, Rita refused "the sexy see-norita roles. And that wasn't easy 'cause that was all that was offered me; easy, ignorant, illiterate, and needy women. It was almost pornographic." Rita needed to draw on inner strength as she continued to fight racism, sexism, and eventually, ageism.

Although Moreno was fiery and formidable on screen, off-screen she was a hot mess. In 1954, in a makeup room on the set of Marlon Brando's *Desiree*, in which he played Napoleon, the twenty-two-year-old Moreno met the man who impacted her life. In *Rita Moreno: A Memoir*, she recalled, "Just meeting him that first day sent my body temperature skyrocketing as though I had been dropped into a very hot bath, and I went into a full-body blush. It was the sort of rush that inspires poetry and songs." However, their torrid, eight-year affair inspired chronic philandering, emotional abuse, a botched abortion, and a suicide attempt. Part of the problem was that Brando had "insatiable sexual needs" that made him pursue numerous other women. During their relationship, he married twice and fathered children with his wives. Yet Rita could not stay away from the notorious narcissist; she became addicted to the challenge of winning him over and over again. In a move as old as relationships, Rita decided to win Marlon back through the jealousy card, and took up with a disappointing Dennis Hopper and the British critic Kenneth Tynan, who turned into her stalker. During a particularly rough patch with Brando—she had discovered a nightie in his closet—

Moreno read in a gossip column that Elvis Presley wanted to meet her. Her Presley dates ended in a tender tussle with Elvis' pelvis moving in that famous gyration, but that was it, folks. One day, watching the King devour a peanut butter, banana, and bacon sandwich, Rita realized he could not compete, and she returned to Marlon. The reunion resulted in a pregnancy; Brando immediately arranged for an abortion and for his friend to pick her up post-operation. The doctors botched the procedure, and to her horror, the stillborn fetus remained inside. Marlon's response was less than empathetic; he swore he would get his money back from the doctor. The straw that finally broke Rita's back was when he married Tarita Teriipaia. Distraught, she took an overdose of sleeping pills. Of the desperate act, she recalled, "I went to bed to die. This wasn't a revenge suicide, but a consolation, an escape-from-pain death." She recovered and, through her therapist's intervention, finally ended her corrosive relationship. At this juncture, a friend set Rita up with Jewish cardiologist Lenny Gordon, and they remained together until his 2010 death. Marriage and motherhood gave her the strength to resist falling back into Brando's arms. After Marlon's death, the only piece of movie memorabilia in his Mulholland Drive home was a photo of him locked in a passionate embrace with a nude Moreno.

The lyric from Gloria Gaynor's "I Will Survive"—"I used to cry but now I hold my head up high"—represents Rita's metamorphosis from Rosa to a strong, independent woman. Currently, the octogenarian is as much a spitfire as ever, and proudly proclaims that in her eighth decade, she has hit her prime, saying, "I am the happiest eighty-two-year-old person I know." In the latter part of life, she has finally been able to put behind her the trauma of the separation from her father and brother, societal prejudice, and the monomaniacal Brando relationship. Unfortunately, even her forty-six-year marriage turned out to be a sham. It transpired that Rita had been an actress both on stage and off, and revealed her husband had been tyrannical and possessive, monitoring her every move.

His controlling behavior made her feel claustrophobic and explains a comment she once made that she would rather "eat glass than ever get married again." When Gordon passed away, she finally found her freedom; the guise of a happy wife was a long-standing role. Of it, she said, "It was an astonishing discovery. After all the years of supervision, I can do whatever I want. It was a very long time to be that unhappy."

In 2014, Moreno was driving near her home in Berkeley, California, when she picked up her cell phone; on the other end was the head of the Screen Actors Guild with the news that its members had chosen her to receive the Guild's fiftieth Life Achievement Award. A gobsmacked Rita slammed on the brakes and "damn near had an accident." The eighty-two-year-old had not expected the honor, and called back for confirmation that she had not experienced an auditory hallucination. Rita said of the award, "Truly, unless I won the Nobel Prize, I don't know that I can compare it to anything I've experienced—and that does include the Oscar." Her concern was how to phrase her one-minute acceptance speech. "That's going to be extremely difficult. I am Puerto Rican and can't even say hello in a minute." The following year, she added the Kennedy Center Honors to her impressive trophy shelf. Her earlier awards sat in a cardboard box until her late husband intervened. Other mementos in her Berkeley, California, hillside home—where she moved to be closer to daughter Fernanda and her two grandsons—include a Presidential Medal of Honor. A high-profile fan is fellow Puerto Rican, Supreme Court Justice Sonia Sotomayor, who said she was honored to call her a friend, and Moreno was the voice in the audio recording of Sotomayor's 2013 memoir, *My Beloved World*. The actress remains elegant and lithe, and in 2015 was at Rockefeller Center in New York City hawking her new CD, sporting a dark, body-hugging top under a print blouse. However, she admits her knees are shot from all the years of dancing in high heels. She still retains the glamour and sultriness of her 1954 *Life* magazine cover that proclaimed, "Rita Moreno: An Actress's Catalog of Sex and Innocence." Still going as strong as ever, Ms. Moreno said she is as happy as an uneaten clam, and in her later years, she is having the time of her life. She quipped of her ability to not define herself by the year on her birth certificate, "I should be a representative for AARP!"

In 2018, the living legend teamed up with Norman Lear for a remake of the director's 1970s classic sitcom *One Day at a Time*—with a Latin twist. Subsequently, the powerhouses arrived at the Golden Globes on a scooter built for two, where the 86-year-old Rita rocked form-fitting leather pants. Although she caught the attention of everyone on the red carpet, the *New York Times* disrespected her when it referred to Ms. Moreno as Mr. Lear's guest. Fans immediately fired back on social media, thereby proving the esteem in which America holds the iconic star. Lear poked fun at the firestorm when he tweeted: "The Rita Moreno and guest." The outrage was understandable, as Ms. Moreno is one of only four actors to have earned the grand slam of show business by winning an EGOT: Emmy, Grammy, Oscar, Tony. Latinos revere Moreno as a role model and call her "La Pioneer." The star is also a longtime civil rights activist who was with Dr. Martin Luther King, Jr. during his "I Have a Dream" speech.

In *West Side Story*, Maria was affiliated with the Puerto Rican gang the Sharks; however, considering the upward trajectory of her life, she is their rival, the Jets.

CHAPTER TWENTY-THREE

Live Long and Prosper (1932)

A half century ago, *Star Trek* pledged "to boldly go where no one had gone before." The tagline, played before every episode, referred to the exploration of space—the final frontier. With a black female star and a Russian hero in a 1960s America filled with racial and Cold War tensions, the television show dealt with more than intergalactic worlds.

The woman also destined to boldly go where no one had gone before was born in Robbins, Illinois, near Chicago, as Grace Dell. Even as a fetus, she had an extraordinary life. Her mother, Lishia, was pregnant when Al Capone's brother paid a less than cordial visit to her father, Samuel Nichols, the town's mayor. The mobster's agenda entailed a hit on Nichols for destroying Capone's alcohol mill, although the mob had been paying for him to turn a blind eye. The henchman spared Sam's life when he discovered the truth: Nichols had not received a cent because he would never have allowed booze in his town. The mobster even let him live when he saw Lishia had placed a pillow over her bulging belly to hide the gun she would have used had the mob killed her husband. The family's second brush with infamy occurred in 1997, when son Thomas Nichols became one of the thirty-nine members of Heaven's Gate who committed mass suicide in San Diego, undertaken in the wake of the Hale-Bopp comet. In an emotional interview on *Larry King Live,* Grace, (later known as Nichelle), said her family had lost contact with her brother twenty years earlier.

The performing bug bit Grace at an early age, and after her days in high school, she danced at the Sherman House

Hotel. One astounding perk was meeting some of the great names of the entertainment world, such as Lena Horne, Ella Fitzgerald, and Josephine Baker. At this time, she also decided she did not care for the name Grace and took her mother's suggestion to change it to Nichelle, as it was alliterative with Nichols, and for its derivative of Victorious Maiden.

At age seventeen, Nichelle was hungry for autonomy and believed she had found it with dancer Foster Johnson, fifteen years her senior. Infatuated, she said that on stage he could make Fred Astaire look like he was standing still, and he was so charming he could talk flowers off wallpaper. In reality, he was a narcissist, a character trait the teenaged Nichelle mistakenly chalked up to artistic temperament. Aware her parents would veto the relationship, she purposefully became pregnant, and after their wedding, Nichelle and Foster moved to Ohio. The bloom of romance withered, as Nichelle did not approve of his alcohol and drug use. Although the marriage collapsed, it produced Nichelle's only child, Kyle, who she referred to as the greatest accomplishment of her life. When her mother called to say Duke Ellington wanted to hire her, she flew back to Chicago and performed with his band.

In 1962, Nichelle fell for Gene Roddenberry; the fly in the romantic ointment was his marital status, though he offered the cliché that he was only staying for the sake of his children. She felt that, even if he did divorce, another impediment would be condemnation of an interracial couple. The situation came to a head when Gene introduced Nichelle to Majel Barrett, his other girlfriend. Nichelle refused to be the other woman to the other woman, and left to work in Paris. There she received a telegram from her agent telling her to fly home immediately; there was a promising role for her in a new television series.

In a move light-years ahead of its time, Roddenberry's vision for his television series was a twenty-third-century world that reflected his contemporary one, and he wanted to make a key member of the Starship Enterprise a black woman. During her interview, a studio executive commented on the book she was holding, entitled *Uhura* (Swahili for "freedom"), and Lieutenant Nyota Uhura became Nichelle's *Star Trek* name. Her character was not a glorified intergalactic telephone operator: She was the head of the *Enterprise* communications and a top graduate of the Starfleet Academy, a protégée of Spock. A black woman who had the responsibilities of a bridge crew officer, even in the fictional setting of space, was unheard of in the TV landscape of the 1960s, and it came with collateral damage. Nichelle was thrilled with the prospect of a regular paycheck that would allow her to finally spend time with her son, buy her mother a house, and trade in her old Renault. However, when the bigwigs discovered Uhura's role was to be more than eye-candy in a form-fitting red minidress, whose lines were to extend beyond, "Yes, Captain!" they ordered Gene to fire her. Their concern was that the network affiliates in the Deep South would cancel the show. Gene refused to comply, and the compromise was that Nichelle worked on an as-needed basis. Further acts of racism occurred with slights, comments such as that the studio would be better off with a blue-eyed blonde, and the withholding of fan mail. Nichelle, having arm-wrestled Jim Crow for years, told Roddenberry she was disembarking from the Enterprise. His response was that, if she did so, then the racists would have won; however, she took the view that, if she stayed to be treated as less of a person than her coworkers, the racists would have won. In either contingency, she was no longer willing to wage this war.

The following evening, Nichelle attended an NAACP fundraising event in Beverly Hills, where a man informed her that a big fan wanted to meet Uhura. She was speechless when the Trekkie turned out to be Dr. Martin Luther King, Jr., who told her that *Star Trek* was the only show he and Coretta allowed their children to stay up to watch. When she informed him that she was quitting, he used his considerable power of oratory to point out that, in the streets, the police were fire-hosing African-Americans for wanting to sit down in a whites-only restaurant, while she was portraying an astronaut of the twenty-third century. He argued that Uhura was inspirational, and hers was the only black portrayal on television in a worthwhile role. He continued, "Here we are marching, and there you are, projecting where we're going." His argument proved prescient. Caryn Elaine Johnson (later Whoopi Goldberg) remembered watching the show as a nine-year-old who yelled, "Momma, there's a black lady on TV and she ain't no maid!" On Monday morning, Nichelle rescinded her resignation. Upon relating the event that had changed her mind, Roddenberry replied, "God bless Dr. Martin Luther King. Somebody does understand me." A month later, Nichelle sang at the slain civil rights leader's funeral.

One of the most groundbreaking shows of the *Star Trek* series was 1968's "Plato's Stepchildren," which featured a kiss where no kiss had gone before. The interracial smooch was between Captain Kirk (who had a girl in every port of every planet) and Uhura. To offset any repercussions in the South, the plot made the couple unwilling lovers, made to embrace by a psychokinetic alien villain, Parmen. Asked if she enjoyed the dozens of takes the scene entailed, Uhura, ever the lady, refused to kiss and tell. The episode received more fan mail than ever, mostly positive. In her autobiography, *Beyond Uhura*, she quoted one of the fan letters that William Shatner shared with her: "I'm a white Southern gentleman, and I like *Star Trek*. I am totally opposed to the mixing of the races. However, any time a red-blooded American boy like Captain Kirk gets a beautiful dame in his arms that looks like Uhura, he ain't gonna fight it."

The USS Enterprise's warp drive drew to a halt in 1969, the end of a TV era. At the same time, Nichelle married Duke Mondy; however, their mutual love of music was not enough to salve their differences, and they divorced several years later.

Nichols went on to star as Uhura in the first six *Star Trek* films until 1991, by which time she was in her mid-fifties. Although she retired the miniscule red dress, retirement was not in the stars for its owner. In 1975, she attended a Chicago convention that attracted thirty thousand Trekkies; also in attendance was Dr. von Puttkamer, NASA's distinguished representative. Asked why he had come to an event celebrating a TV show, he answered that what made the sci-fi series so critical was its sense that "the universe is worth living in, the equality of men and women in peaceful exploration, knowing we are better than what we think we are. It is not even that." Then he added, "What I have come here for today is to find out for myself if Miss Uhura's legs are as beautiful in person as they appear on the TV screen." In *Beyond Uhura,* Nichelle did not say how she reacted to the good doctor's words, but the presence of NASA led to another frontier. In the 1980s, Nichelle worked for the space program as an ambassador with a focus on recruiting minority and women astronauts. Her efforts were instrumental and, like the USS Enterprise's subsequent flights into space, carried females and African-Americans. Dr. Mae Jemison, an African-American member of the Discovery Space Mission, told Nichelle that seeing Uhura when she was young had inspired her to seek a career in space.

The trajectory of Ms. Nichols' life had taken her far afield from Robbins; she had been a guest of Prince Andrew and his then wife Fergie, graced *Ebony Magazine*'s 1967 cover, and was a guest of Trekkie Barack Obama, who posed with her as they both gave the Vulcan salute. (The Chief Executive also confessed to having had a crush on her in his younger years.) In 1992, the fifty-nine-year-old Nichols became the first black entertainer to place her hands in the cement at Grauman's (now Mann's) Chinese Theater in Hollywood. However, never one to rest on her laurels, Nichelle had her eyes on another quest. Even in her eighties, she is not one to repeat her TV closing line, "This communication channel is now closed. Uhura out."

In the 1967 episode "The Deadly Years," the effects of radiation caused the crew of the Enterprise to age at an accelerated rate; this terrified Uhura, as growing old was her greatest fear. In this manner, the fictional and non-fictional took divergent paths, as Nichelle met age with her characteristic aplomb. At age eighty-seven, Nichelle is still glamorous and impeccably dressed, ready to go at warp speed after recovery from a stroke.

In her eighth decade, Ms. Nichols has gone up in space on board NASA's C-141 Astronomy Observatory, which analyzed the atmospheres of Mars and Saturn. She is also still acting, and garnered praise for her role as the aging mother on the soap opera *The Young and the Restless.* For her eighty-fifth birthday, there was a fan meet-and-greet in Los Angeles. When asked what she wanted for her birthday, she replied, "All I want is my two front teeth. Well, I have all my teeth..I just want to keep on keeping on. I love what I do." And to a reporter who asked if she ever planned to stop working, she responded, "Getting tired of work is like getting tired of breathing. The only time I will retire is to a casket."

For integrating the USS Enterprise and NASA, for standing up to racism, and for resisting the onslaught of age, let's raise our hands in the Vulcan salute in honor of Nichelle and repeat their words of farewell, "Live long and prosper."

CHAPTER TWENTY-FOUR

A Room of One's Own (1933)

Ever since Adam and Eve covered their naked bodies, Judeo-Christian society has equated carnality with sin. In this vein, Corinthians admonished that it is better to marry than to burn, and Hester Prynne wore the scarlet letter A, so her Puritan neighbors would know her as an adulteress. William Blake mourned this repression in "The Garden of Love," when he wrote, "And priests in black gowns, were walking their rounds/And binding with briars, my joys and desires." One lady, late in life, determined to disregard "Thou shalt not."

In 1962, Helen Gurley Brown published *Sex and the Single Girl;* in the 1990s, Monica Lewinsky exposed Sex and the Married President; and in 2004, Jane Juska revealed Sex and the Senior. Jane Murback was born in Ann Arbor, Michigan, to father Edwin, a doctor, and mother Helen, a homemaker. The family relocated to Archbold, a small Ohio town, where many neighbors were Mennonites. Jane struggled for years to shed her Puritanical upbringing, and she eventually realized that "Pleasure was not bad." She graduated from the University of Michigan with a degree in English, and at a young age, she married Joe Juska, an employee of the federal government. The union produced only two positive results: an alliterative name and a son, Andrew. Her husband belittled her and "wanted me to collapse intellectually. Whether the topic was the weather, politics or rent, he was always argumentative." After their divorce in the early 1970s, Jane moved to the more liberal zip code of Berkeley. Although she did not mourn the breakup, she said the loneliest she had ever been was when she was married, and she went through a bleak period. Juska gained seventy pounds, drank heavily, and was beside herself when Andrew dropped out of school and ran away from home. Jane underwent years of psychoanalysis, dieting, and mother-son reunion to quiet her demons. To support herself, Juska taught English for more than three decades at Ygnacio Valley High School, Saint Mary's College, and San Quentin State Prison. In her spare time, she escorted women into abortion clinics to shield them from pro-life protestors. Dating was sporadic, and except for a couple of unhappy skirmishes, her relationships with men were nonexistent. Overwhelmed with making a living and raising a child on her own, she did not want to add a romantic complication into the mix.

Jane's salvation had been her passion for teaching; however, after she retired, she found she "just wasn't tired enough," and, with Andrew gone (he became a forester), it dawned on her that she had gone three decades without sex. She tried to end the drought; however, despite senior hikes, senior birdwatching, senior mixes, and senior dances at church (which she no longer attended), by 7:00 p.m., she was alone and lonely.

At age sixty-six, Jane watched the French film *Autumn Tale*, a story in which a married woman secretly placed a personal advertisement in a newspaper for a widowed friend who believed it too late to find love. The film made a significant impact, leading Jane to reflect both on her enforced celibacy and her sadness that she had never realized her dream of publishing a book. Jane was determined to do something about the former, and this determination was the genesis of taking out a personal ad. First, she consulted Andrew, the only person's censure about which she cared. His response, "Go get 'em, Mom. It's your turn." Her grandmother had warned her, "Don't borrow trouble," but she felt borrowing trouble was a good idea because "if you live your life staying safe, you're going to lose."

Of course, the retired schoolteacher was cognizant of the risks, as putting herself in the meeting-strangers arena could equate to *Looking for Mr. Goodbar,* but she felt an emotional death was no longer sustainable. Desirous of meeting a literary gentleman, she bought an ad in the personals section of the *New York Review of Books.* At the cost of $4.55 per word, she cut to the chase: "Before I turn sixty-seven next March, I would like a lot of sex with a man I like. If you want to talk first, Trollope works for me." Jane had debated about mentioning the British writer, as it added thirty dollars to the cost, yet left it in, as she felt it would establish her as an intellectual.

Juska expected two or three responses; sixty-three replies landed on her doormat, from men ranging from thirty-two to eighty-five, forwarded by the *New York Review* in manila envelopes. She divided these into piles of yes, no, and maybe; only those from men on life-support machines or with little sense of literary appreciation made the no pile. One man mailed a picture of himself wearing sunglasses and nothing else (Jane did not reply); another bore the message, "Have Viagra, will travel." The letters yielded several dates which in turn yielded sexual encounters.

Like any dater, her experiences ran from the sublime to the ridiculous. In the latter category was Jonah, an eighty-something, and they shared a rendezvous at the Claremont Hotel. It ended with him stealing the champagne flutes and her silk pajama pants. John proved the proverbial charmer, as she found his literary foreplay irresistible: "Margaret Fuller. Margaret Atwood. Roth. Updike." She spent a great deal of time and money travelling to the East Coast to meet dates because California guys did not pique her interest. She said the problem was not impotence or prostate problems; rather, her bone of contention was their lack of appreciation for the metaphysical poetry of John Donne. Jane fell in love with one of her paramours, Graham, or, as he called himself, Abelard, half her age, who had the body of an Adonis. For him, she

disregarded the cardinal rule "Bros before hoes"—at least
its female equivalent—when she broke arrangements with
Meredith, her oldest friend, to spend a weekend with her
Lysander in a log cabin.

After a year of living the sexual life, Jane decided to turn
another fantasy into reality, and she set her sights on seeing
her name on the spine of a book. Without any publishing
connections, Mrs. Juska sent out her randy read. The top-
rated William Morris Agency signed her on as a client. The
book's goal was to dispel the common misconception that
postmenopausal women were not interested in the pleasures
of the flesh, even if their flesh no longer possessed elasticity.
Her 2003 memoir carried the title *A Round-Heeled Woman: My
Late-Life Adventures in Sex and Romance*; the name an archaic
reference to a trollop, not Trollope, the British writer. The book
is noticeable not only for its frankness about the intricacies
of senior love, but also for the author's honesty about her
naked need for a physical relationship. Juska's carnal odyssey
was a precursor to E. L. James's 2011 *Fifty Shades of Grey*,
though Jane's gray referred to lack of pigment, rather than a
billionaire who was into bondage. Jane's memoir, a bestseller
on both sides of the Atlantic, landed her on the *Oprah Winfrey
Show*. Oprah's guest, with white hair tucked behind her ears,
eyes alert behind her bifocals, was not the usual woman
behind a sexual sensation. Juska kept clutching her back, and
one assumed it was from arthritis until one remembered
her extra-curricular activities. When another interviewer
asked her if she practiced safe sex, Jane answered, "Well, not
getting pregnant was part of my popularity." The memoir also
became the basis of a play performed in several cities. Legions
read the best -seller, except Andrew, because it contained
too much information about his mother's life. It must also
have provoked a great deal of staff-room conversation in her
former schools, especially in the Catholic College. In a nod to
changing the names to protect the innocent, Juska exercised
discretion, and her boy toys became Danny the Priest, Jonah
the Thief, Robert the Liar, and Sidney the Peculiar. Andrew

said in an interview that he'd never read the book, and then added that, if someone else's mother had written it, he would have done so.

After her book's debut, elderly fans lionized the retired schoolteacher who found herself in the unlikely role of sex guru for a generation of wrinkled baby boomers. Her story, however graphic, was about more than the pleasures of the flesh, in the same way that Melville's *Moby Dick* was about more than a madman's quest for a white whale. It dealt with the need of seniors for connection, and how solitude is a gateway to death-in-life.

Mrs. Juska was an author in search of a sequel, and her second book was *Unaccompanied Women: Late-Life Adventures in Love, Sex, and Real Estate,* which described her reinvented life as a seventy-two-year-old "senior sexpert." It recounted her search for the perfect rental property (she lusted after her friends' homes and longingly dreamed of owning her own). Her rented Berkeley cottage was too small and too expensive, and she worried the owners would be so shocked at her screams of Miltonian fulfillment, they would ask her to vacate. Man-hunting proved no less problematic, and she remained on the hunt for sex and romance, though she could not find anyone sexually compatible and six feet tall within a three-thousand-mile radius. Graham, her thirty-two-year-old New York City intellectual love, informed her via email that he had married a woman his age. Robert, her second favorite, ran off with her friend Ilse. Ms. Juska said of her heartache, "And I would like to say that that experience is no easier at sixty-seven than it is at seventeen. It's just at sixty-seven, one has less time to get over it." Jane's irrepressible humor offset any sadness. Her 2015 book was the novel she had always wanted to pen, *Mrs. Bennet Has Her Say,* which examined the marriage of the parents of the heroine of *Pride and Prejudice.*

Critics hailed Juska's books as taboo-busters and readers—at least those in her liberal Berkeley zip code (not so much her childhood Mennonite neighbors) —reveled in senior sexual liberation. The ladies in her gym took the radical in their midst in stride; in the San Francisco Bay area, the only unforgivable sin is to be on the wrong side of the political spectrum. Jane addressed this issue: "If they found out that I was Republican, say, I would be shunned immediately." From a stylistic perspective, Jane proved herself as polished a writer as she was a speaker. In the wrong hands, her years of living dangerously could have degenerated into the trashiest of California New Age jargon or a sordid sexual manual for the over-sixty crowd. As a resident of California, an interviewer asked her the inevitable question: If her book became a film, who would she cast in the starring roles? When he suggested Judi Dench as Ms. Juska, Jane shook her head. She said she would play herself and that Daniel Day-Lewis would play her men—all of them. The final question was if there would be further ads, or if she was finally putting the brakes on her correspondence. Jane's reply: "Who knows? Maybe in ten years. Well, let me see. That would get me to eighty. Well, why not?"

But, between the lines, dealing with lust crept in a note of *Bonjour Tristesse.* Her lonesome kvetching—even in the guise of humor—left singletons, regardless of age, a trifle blue. Ms. Juska concluded that life is random, romance and sex are fleeting, and older women will always be marginalized. Jane's erotic journey may have started with Trollope, but it ended with Hardy. Juska wrote that, in retrospect, she finally understood the last line of *The Mayor of Casterbridge,* "Happiness was but the occasional episode in a general drama of pain." However, her late-in-life sexploits were not in vain. In a nod to Virginia Woolf (a literary reference Ms. Juska would have appreciated), with the windfall from her books she was, at long last, able to afford a room of her own.

CHAPTER TWENTY-FIVE

The Book of Ruth (1933)

In the 1960s, Diana Ross, sheathed in sequined splendor, belted out hits for Motown's The Supremes. A half-century later, there appeared another Supreme—one dressed in black with a distinctive collar—who dissented in DC.

Nathan and Celia Bader fled Europe to escape anti-Semitism and settled in Flatbush, Brooklyn, where he worked as a furrier, providing a luxury good not in demand during the Great Depression. In addition to straitened circumstances, the family encountered anti-Semitism; on a drive through Pennsylvania, Nathan and Celia saw a resort with a sign: "No dogs or Jews allowed." Their older daughter Marylin nicknamed little sister Ruth "Kiki" from the expression that she was a "kicky baby." The first of the family's tragedies occurred when Marylin passed away at age six from meningitis.

At Madison High, Ruth proved to be a leader, editing the school newspaper, where she wrote articles on the Bill of Rights, and serving as an officer in the Go-Getters, a club for social events. She chipped her tooth twirling a baton when Madison played Lincoln High. Ruth, although slated for valedictorian, did not attend her high school graduation, as her mother had died two days before from ovarian cancer.

At Cornell University, Ruth majored in government, and credits Professor Cushman with igniting her interest in law. The era was the heyday of McCarthyism, and Cushman taught how words can fight injustice. Another important influence was her European literature teacher, Vladimir Nabokov, who honed Ruth's skills as a writer. To no one's surprise, Bader graduated with high honors.

Diana Ross sang, "Whenever you're near I hear a symphony, a tender melody," and Ruth felt this way about Martin David Ginsburg, a year ahead of her at Cornell, whom she met on a blind date in 1951. Her initial attraction: "Marty was an unusual man. In fact, he was the first boy I knew who cared that I had a brain." Three years later, they married; on their wedding day, her mother-in-law advised her with the memorable words, "In every good marriage, it helps sometimes to be a little deaf." In a move uncommon for the era, Ruth continued to work even after the arrival of her daughter Jane and son James. What also helped was that Marty proved the incarnation of Sheryl Sandburg's dictum that the most important career choice you'll make is who you marry. Ruth's culinary skills were not her strong suit, and Marty became the chef supreme. When they lived in an apartment in The Watergate, they hosted regular dinner parties, where Marty produced meals with the same meticulous zeal he used in his legal career. The recipe that garnered the most glowing reviews from his wife was the very un-kosher pork loin braised in milk. So equal were Marty and Ruth's roles that James always wondered why people would only ask what his father did for a living. Above all, Marty gave his wife the gift of confidence. Ruth said of her spouse, "He always made me feel like I was better than I thought myself."

Despite antiquated views about the role of women in society in the 1950s, Ruth followed her husband to Harvard Law. There were only nine women in the class of five hundred, and at a dinner party, the Dean asked the women how they justified taking a place in the student body that should have gone to a man. Despite the demands of raising two children and nursing her husband through a bout of testicular cancer, Ruth earned a place on the Harvard Law Review. In 1958, Martin accepted a position with a prominent New York City firm, and Ruth transferred to Columbia. Although classmates considered her "the smartest person on the East Coast," she nevertheless found it impossible to obtain employment. Ginsburg explained in a 1993 interview, "In the fifties, the traditional law firms were just beginning to turn around on hiring Jews.. But to be a woman, a Jew, and a mother to boot, that combination was a bit much." Instead, prospective firms asked about her typing skills. The five-foot-tall, 100-pound pit bull finally found a position and became the second female law professor at Rutgers University. What tempered her enthusiasm was that the school informed her they would pay her less than her peers because "You have a husband who earns a good salary." In order to keep the position during her second pregnancy, she wore her mother-in-law's loose-fitting clothes. When Columbia changed its policy in 1972, Ruth became the first tenured woman in its law school faculty. Her work for feminist causes earned admiration from Gloria Steinem, and in a note penned on *Ms. Magazine* stationary, she told Ruth that she made her "very, very proud."

Marty, a supportive husband at home, was also a successful tax attorney, growing the Ginsburg fortune to between $10 million and $45 million. He was constantly at Ruth's side during her two occurrences of cancer. He proved the ultimate feminist husband when he said, "I think that the most important thing I have done is enable Ruth to do what she has done." President Carter assigned her to a seat on the US Court of Appeals for the District of Columbia Circuit in 1980, and President Clinton gave her a spot on the Supreme Court in 1993. This appointment made Ruth the second woman, and the first Jewish one, ever nominated to the top bench. When Clinton introduced her to the nation in the White House Rose Garden, he called her "the Thurgood Marshall of gender equality." In her acceptance speech, she said that her mother "was the bravest and strongest person I have known, who was taken from me much too soon. I pray that I may be all that she would have been, had she lived in an age when women could aspire and achieve, and daughters are cherished as much as sons." President Clinton wiped away a tear. The hallowed position did not mean an end to misogyny. When she argued her first case before the Supreme Court, Justice Harry Blackmun rated her a C+ in his diary. ("Very precise female.") Later, Ruth quipped what would have been a fitting rejoinder, saying, "There will be enough women on the Supreme Court when there are nine."

Ruth had not received a law degree from Harvard, even though she had done most of her coursework there, and in 2011, the university offered her an honorary one. Another recipient at this time was Placido Domingo; Ruth was ecstatic, as she loves opera as much as she loves the law. At the ceremony, Domingo broke out in a semi-spontaneous serenade of the Justice he held in the highest esteem. A photograph that captured this memory sits on the mantelpiece in Ginsburg's chambers. She recalls, "It was one of the greatest moments of my life." Another mutual admiration was between Ruth and former President Barack Obama. When he paid a courtesy call to the Justices before his 2009 inauguration, Anthony Kennedy invited him to play basketball in the court's top-floor gym. "I don't know," Obama replied, "I hear that Justice Ginsburg has been working on her jump shot." At the annual Hanukkah celebration at the White House in 2011, Obama noted, "Justice Ruth Bader Ginsburg is here. We are thrilled to see her. She's one of my favorites. I've got a soft spot for Justice Ginsburg." Beside the photograph of Ruth and Placido is another of Obama embracing Ruth at a State of the Union address.

To help keep her body fit, Ruth pumps iron in the Supreme Court's ground-level gym with a personal trainer who used to be an Army parachutist. Her favorite snack indulgence: prunes. Outside of court, she is a fashionista. Her elegant jabots have gained notoriety, she has a weakness for Ferragamo shoes, and, on occasion, she has rocked a turban. RBG also often wears black or white lace gloves on her hands of steel.

However, not everyone is in Court Ruth. During Donald Trump's campaign, she took off her gloves and called him a "faker" and said that, if her husband were alive, he would view a Trump victory as "time for us to move to New Zealand." The president-elect appeared to view the black-robed justice with the same disdain. Trump tweeted his response by writing, "Justice Ginsburg of the US Supreme Court has embarrassed all by making very dumb political statements about me. Her mind is shot—resign!" Ruth refrained from further comment; after all, sometimes it helps to be a little deaf. Although, at age eighty-five, resigning is not something on Ruth's agenda. She said, "I will do this job as long as I feel that I can do it full steam. As long as I have the candlepower, I will do it. At my age, you have to take it year by year. So this year I know I'm fine. What will be next year or the next year? I can't predict." Ginsburg fans view RBG as one of the final defenses against a conservative agenda. For this reason, a *Washington Post* columnist told Ginsburg, "If you have any need for blood, you can have the eight or so units of A-positive that are right here in my body. There's also a gently used liver in here, lobes of it just lying around if you need them." After the election, Ruth wore her dissent collar.

An octogenarian Supreme Court Justice and Jewish grandma seems an unlikely choice for Internet stardom, yet she has far exceeded Warhol's fifteen minutes of fame. Her acclaim is an ode to her six-decade extensive career of smashing glass ceilings for women and dissenting against injustice. For the past few years, her bespectacled image has proliferated on social media. The self-proclaimed "flaming feminist litigator" pop-culture status is attributed to Shana Knizhnik, who created a Tumblr, that became a biography, dedicated to Ruth—NOTORIOUS RBG. For those uninitiated into hip-hop, the moniker is a play on the nickname of the three-hundred-pound Brooklyn-born rapper Biggie Smalls, murdered in 1997. The hagiography helped transform a black robe into a red cape. A cottage industry of Ginsburgiana proliferated: greeting cards, Halloween costumes, nail art,

tattoos, needlepoint samplers, and bobbleheads. *Objets de*
Ruth are now part of the temple of highbrow kitsch. Articles
of apparel display her image along with captions like Can't
Spell Truth Without Ruth, Fear the Frill, and Queen Supreme.
Television jumped on the Ginsburg bandwagon, and Ruth
became a recurring character on *Saturday Night Live*'s
"Weekend Update." In 2015, she appeared on the cover of
Time magazine.

Behind the fame and acclaim lies a never-ending
heartache. The man who "never gave her second-class
treatment" developed severe back pain, and doctors identified
a tumor near Marty's spine. In 2010, when Ruth came to visit
her husband at Johns Hopkins Hospital, she opened a drawer
next to his bed and saw a yellow legal pad.

> *My dearest Ruth—You are the only person I have loved
> in my life, setting aside, a bit, parents and kids and their
> kids, and I have admired and loved you almost since the
> day we first met at Cornell some fifty-six years ago. What
> a treat it has been to watch you progress to the very top of
> the legal world!!*

MARTY

Her beloved husband passed away at their home on
June 27. The next morning, Justice Ginsburg was on the
bench to read an opinion on the final day of the Court's term.
Her explanation of the abbreviated grieving period: "That's
because Marty would have wanted it."

The Supreme Court will forever bear the fingerprint
of RBG, as her liberal rulings made America stand by its
democratic ideals. From Brooklyn to the Bench makes for a
fascinating story in *The Book of Ruth*.

CHAPTER TWENTY-SIX

Special Place in Hell (1937)

The word "secretary" sometimes carries negative connotations; it conjures an image of a subordinate female whose job description entails typing, bringing coffee, and taking shorthand. These Girl Fridays combine the requisite traits of efficiency and self-effacement, the unsung minions. In contrast, when "secretary" bears a capital letter, it denotes a pinnacle of power.

The woman who put the preface "extra" before the word "ordinary" was Marie Jana, the daughter of the diplomat Josef Korbelova and his wife Mandula. In 1939, the family fled Prague after the Nazi invasion, and took refuge in England. They survived the Blitz and returned to their homeland after Germany's defeat. Three years later, the family escaped once more in the wake of the Communist coup that snuffed out Czechoslovak democracy. This time, they sought asylum in the United States, which became their permanent residence. Josef obtained a position as the Dean of the University of Denver's School of International Studies; one of his students was Condoleezza Rice. Eager to assimilate, Josef shortened their name to Korbel; Marie Jana went by the name Madeleine. She attended Wellesley College and majored in political science, even though few opportunities were available in the '50s for girls aspiring to a career in this field.

What lessened the sting was meeting Prince Disarming—Joseph Medill Patterson Albright, the possessor of three surnames and a stratospheric family fortune—when both had summer jobs at the *Denver Post*. He was a scion of media royalty; his great-aunt Cissy Patterson had been the owner

of the *Washington-Times Herald*. Although Madeleine had
a difficult time winning over his well-connected parents,
he proposed six weeks later, and they married after her
graduation. In the vein of Henry IV—Paris was worth a
mass—Madeleine traded her Roman Catholic religion for the
Albright's Episcopalian church. The romance, she said, made
her feel like Cinderella. Although she had been anxious for a
career, she had also had her eye on the prize of wedlock and
had wanted to get married "as soon as possible to a perfect
partner." The couple's residences were a well-appointed
Georgetown home and a quail-hunting estate in Georgia, the
latter bequeathed to Joseph by his aunt Alicia Patterson.

The publishing prince whisked Madeleine away to a
rarefied zip code, where she gave birth to premature twins,
Alice and Anne, who struggled for life but survived. Six
months into her second pregnancy, Madeleine contracted
German measles, and her doctor warned her the baby was
most likely brain-damaged. A late-term abortion was not
an option, and the infant died at birth. Her last pregnancy
resulted in a healthy daughter, Katherine. Madeleine
reminisced, "A portrait of the Albright family in the mid-'70s
would have shown a happily married couple, with three smart
and beautiful daughters." Madeleine studied for a PhD in
public law and government at Columbia University; the only
way she was able to write her thesis, as the mother of three
(despite hired help), was by rising every morning at 4:30 for
three years. While Joseph forged his career as a journalist, she
followed him from city to city, finally settling in Washington.
As her girls grew older, Madeleine worked as a Democratic
fundraiser, and she eventually found a position in the White
House under the tutelage of her former professor, Zbigniew
Brzezinski, President Carter's national security adviser. When
Ronald Reagan won the next election, Madeleine lost her
position and found herself in the political periphery.

At this juncture, Joseph, her husband of twenty-three
years, dropped what she called a thunderbolt on their gilded

life. While sitting in their living room having coffee, Joe informed Madeleine that their marriage was dead; he had fallen for someone younger and more attractive. The P. S. to the conversation: He was moving out to live in Atlanta, where the woman he loved was a reporter. Madeleine wrote in her biography that she did not know what had upset her most: that Joe had presented her with a done deal, that he had said she had become too old-looking, or that he could not see why she was so upset. Joseph left that afternoon, but developed misgivings about his decision and kept calling his wife to inform her of his daily feelings: "I love you 60 percent and her 40 percent." Then, the next day: "I love her 70 percent and you 30 percent." The Albrights attempted a reconciliation with a ski trip to Aspen, where Joseph complemented Madeleine on her weight loss, a result of the Diet Center plus the looming specter of divorce. She recalled that she skied better than at any other time, "Perhaps because I didn't particularly care if I broke my neck." Any hope of a reunion soon vanished. The Pulitzer Prize was looming—an award Joseph had long coveted—and he offered the proposition that, if he won, he would stay, as he would not want a marital scandal to tarnish his achievement. The woman who would one day tell Fidel Castro that he had no *cojones* rolled over and took it. As it turned out, the Albright marriage would have survived had the Pulitzer committee made a different decision. When Joseph went AWOL, what was a middle-aged matron to do? (1) Take one of the priceless pieces of bric-a-brac to the family jewel, thus ending the other woman's appeal; (2) Book an appointment with Dr. Kevorkian; or (3) Become a contemporary Miss Havisham. Madeleine felt she was floundering in the middle of an ocean *sans* life-preserver. She said of her abyss of loneliness, "I had tried the glass slipper, and it had fit. In the fairytale, that is where the story ends. In life, it is merely the beginning of a new chapter." The wife scorned had to navigate uncharted territory as she figured out her new romantic life, a difficult feat as she had not looked at a man other than her husband since she was twenty. Moreover, she had no self-confidence, thanks to Joe's parting comments about her looks. She said she had no idea of the dating arena and felt like a forty-five-year-old virgin. Pulling herself up by the proverbial bootstraps, she decided her best course of action was to fill her time, and to move quickly because the ice under her was so thin. Succor came, not in the arms of another man, but rather by leaning on female friends, developing self-reliance, and by an extremely generous settlement. Eventually, she "no longer felt like an egg without a shell."

In a nod to there being life after loss, Madeleine found an outlet as a professor at Georgetown University and pursued a further foray into politics. From there, she went into foreign policy and fundraising, finding, as she rose through the ranks that male colleagues regarded the female interloper with suspicion. She soon transformed herself into a leading authority on international diplomacy and rose to prominence as the US Ambassador to the United Nations. Despite her lofty title, the predominantly male press corps deemed her not in the same league as her testosterone-charged predecessors. A reporter wrote that women are just too emotional to do the job, and it was a running joke to refer to Albright as Half-Bright. Despite the slights, Madeleine soldiered on. During her ambassadorship, she famously celebrated Bill Clinton's election victory by swinging her hips and clutching her buttocks in the Security Council chamber to the tune of "La Macarena."

A dozen years after her divorce, Madeleine became the most powerful female official in American history when President Clinton appointed her, at age sixty, Secretary of State, thereby making her the first woman to hold the august appointment. The move shattered a powerful glass ceiling. The aforementioned reporter, her personal Lex Luthor, dismissed her appointment as left-wing political correctness, claiming she only received the post because of her sex: "Window dressing for the Clinton administration." At least former Secretary of State Henry Kissinger was polite when he learned a woman was walking in his old shoes. "Welcome to the fraternity," he said, to which she shot back, "Henry, I hate to tell you, but it's not a fraternity anymore." In her autobiography, *Madame Secretary*, published at age sixty-six, she wrote that, despite meetings with kings and presidents and overseeing treaties, she could not separate gender from her job. Case in point, a to-do list: (1) Call Senator Helms. (2) Call King Hussein. (3) Call Foreign Minister Moussa. (4) Congressional calls. (5) Prepare for China meeting. (6) Buy nonfat yogurt. In the book's pages, she provides a feminist perspective on foreign affairs, explaining, "If women leaders had acted the way Arafat and Barak did during Camp David, they would have been dismissed as menopausal."

For all her success, politically and as a feminist, the most telling moment in her book is her questioning whether a married woman with full domestic responsibilities could ever be the player she had been on the world stage, had she remained a wife. "When I became the Secretary of State, I realized that I would never have climbed that high had I still been married. Yet I am deeply saddened to have been divorced. I know that, at the time, I would have given up any thought of a career if it would have made Joe change his mind." She ruminated that, after a private dinner with Hillary Clinton and the recently widowed Queen Noor of Jordan, Albright calculated the impact of their marriages on each woman. "In different ways we had each been left to explore the boundaries of our own inner strength by a husband who had deceived, deserted, or died."

Just as President Reagan was known for the jar of his omnipresent jelly beans on his Oval Office desk, Madeleine Albright was known for her brooches. Her collection of three-dimensional emojis carried messages. In 1990, she learned the Russians had bugged a conference room near her State Department office, and at her next meeting with Russian diplomats, she sported a huge insect pin. They got the message. When the Iraqi media compared her to an "unparalleled serpent," she displayed a snake pin at her next meeting. An exhibition and book entitled *Read My Pins*—an allusion to the first President Bush's "Read My Lips" —are dedicated to this vast array.

Despite an event-filled life as the Secretary of State, something that hit Madeleine on a visceral level was when the *Washington Post* revealed the Korbels had not been Catholic Czechs. Rather, they had been Jews, and three of her grandparents had perished in Nazi death camps. Critics implied that her shocked response was voluntary amnesia, and that she had knowingly concealed the truth. When asked if she would revert to Judaism, she replied, "I was raised a Christian. Now that I'm sixty-six, why would I suddenly change who I am?"

Today, life is anything but quiet for the octogenarian. The New York Stock Exchange elected her as a member, she launched an investment firm, and she is the chairperson of The Hague Institute for Global Justice. Albright is far too busy to nurse regrets, except the one that has no expiration date— the loss of her husband. Still single, she told her daughters her only requirement in dating: "I can't go out with a Republican."

Madeleine Albright, the refugee who rose to the highest ranks, has as many memorable quotations as she does brooches. Perhaps the greatest of these was her pronouncement, "There's a special place in Hell for women who don't help each other."

CHAPTER TWENTY-SEVEN

Atticus Finch (1937)

Shakespeare's *As You Like It* uses the metaphor of the stage to represent life; everyone is an actor, with entrances and exits. Shakespeare wrote that there are seven stages of existence, from the infant in his nurse's arms to the last scene of all, second childishness—what the Bard called old age. An exception to "second childishness" is an octogenarian whose endless drive and Dorian Gray aging is, like a kaleidoscope, ever beautiful, ever changing.

In *Zelig*, Woody Allen plays the role of a human chameleon who takes on endless incarnations. The non-fictional counterpart to Leonard Zelig was a woman who has performed many roles—actress, activist, author—and was born into Hollywood royalty. However, in a nod to the observation that it is dangerous to let too much light into the castle, the mansion echoed unhappiness. Jane Fonda is the daughter of acclaimed actor Henry and socialite mother Frances, who committed suicide in a psychiatric hospital, probably from manic depression. The tragedy occurred when her daughter was twelve; Henry told her that her mother died from a heart attack, but Jane later learned the truth from a movie magazine. Jane expressed her devastation: "What was left of me could have been put into a thimble." Growing up before the #MeToo movement, Jane suffered a childhood sexual assault in silence. In her memoir, Jane wrote that the emotional fallout from the attack was that she always felt a sense of disembodiment. Healing only took place at age sixty-two, at which time she made peace with her body that had always been a man magnet. For comfort from the dual tragedy, Jane turned to her father, but he was as nurturing as a block of ice. One of the few times he noticed her was when he commented that her legs were too heavy, a partial explanation for later battles with anorexia and bulimia. The young Jane became a broken doll, unable to appreciate that she was beautiful, smart, talented. Not surprisingly, Fonda went looking for love in all the wrong places.

As an eighteen-year-old in France, Fonda met Roger Vadim, who, considering his former relationships with Bridgette Bardot and Catherine Deneuve, exuded high-voltage sexuality. Playing on her insecurities, he convinced her to use her mother's inheritance to pay off his gambling debts, and that her opposition to a *ménage a trois* was bourgeois. Utilizing her considerable acting talent, she faked enjoyment. In order to please him, she turned down starring roles in *Bonnie and Clyde* and *Rosemary's Baby* for *Barbarella*, in which she tossed her hair as well as her vinyl bathing suit, the latter act exposing her beautiful physique. In 1968, Fonda appeared on the cover of *Life* magazine, proclaiming her an international sex symbol. Fonda changed that image with her next project, the Depression-era film *They Shoot Horses Don't They?* Awakened to the decade's activism, Jane felt it time to euthanize her marriage. The blinders dropped from her eyes, and she was no longer willing to put up with Roger's drinking, threesomes, and using her as a walking bank account. The endgame arrived when she espoused causes near and dear to the heart of the '60s, and Roger's response was to dub her Jane of Arc.

Ms. Fonda went into her radical chic phase, learning about black voting rights and the Vietnam War from Marlon Brando. Jane wrote of her nascent activism, "Never underestimate what might be lying dormant beneath the surface of a back-combed blonde wearing false eyelashes." After her hair epiphany, she traded her blonde mane for a brown shag and miniskirt for jeans, and jetted to New Delhi on a solo search for self. Fired with zeal, she then took off to San Francisco to support the takeover of Alcatraz. Squatting in a corner of the former prison yard, she smoked pot with Sioux Indian leaders who were understandably shocked at having a movie star in their midst. As the press focused on Fonda, rather than the plight of the Native Americans, the chief told her she could no longer be their spokesperson, as she did not know enough about the long history of white oppression. Undaunted, she set her sights on the Black Panthers. She lent them her credit card, and they promptly charged a car; she also lost $50,000 when she posted bail for a member who skipped town. The straw that broke Fonda's back was their calling her a "white honkey bitch" and spurious rumors that she was sleeping with their head honcho. In her effort to better the world, she deposited her eighteen-month-old daughter, Vanessa, with Roger, thereby following in her father's misbegotten parenting footsteps. At a feminist consciousness-raising session, she confided, "My biggest regret is I never got to f***Che Guevara."

At this point, Tom Hayden, hair in long braids, made his entrance, and within days, they were making love on the living-room floor. Wanting to live like "the people," the couple moved into a blue-collar neighborhood replete with cockroaches. At the height of her fame in the mid '70s, Jane turned up on the doorstep of her ex-hubby, but not to engage in post-divorce amour. The star of *Klute* and *The China Syndrome* had come to do laundry. Tom had forbidden her to have a washing machine or dishwasher. Hayden tutored his paramour on the Pentagon Papers, and with his support, she travelled alone to North Vietnam, where she was asked to straddle an anti-aircraft gun for a photo-op. When she arrived back in the United States—in coolie hat and Vietnamese pajamas—she did so to the infuriated cries of protestors calling her Hanoi Jane. Even forty-six years later, NBC host Megyn Kelly brought up the hated epithet, though Fonda had issued an endless stream of mea culpas.

The untraditional couple took a traditional turn when they decided to get married in their living room, pungent with the scent of marijuana, while outside the Hell's Angels, friends of her brother, Peter, encircled the house because of death threats. Tom and Jane named their son Troi after Nguyen Van Troi, a Vietcong "martyr" who had tried to assassinate Defense Secretary Robert McNamara. They later changed it to Troy.

Tom began to drink heavily and fooled around with the babysitter while the missus was off filming *Julia*. He stalked out of his wife's screening of *Coming Home*, about a disabled veteran, angry because an actress was getting the spotlight rather than the victims. Jane looked for money to finance her husband's next political campaign and launched an exercise enterprise, *Workout*, that spawned a $20-million fitness program. In lieu of appreciation, Hayden deemed the franchise "an exercise in vanity." Resentment about being called Mr. Fonda ran deep. When Fonda was fifty-one, Hayden announced that, after sixteen years of marriage, he was in love with another woman. What was a two-time Oscar winner to do? Ms. Fonda responded by throwing his belongings out the window in garbage bags. That helped a little, she said.

Jane embarked on her third radical act—as a trophy wife, at age fifty-four—when she took a final walk down the aisle with right-wing billionaire Ted Turner. The lure need not have been his wealth, as she possesses her own $100-million-dollar piggy-bank. His first-date pick-up line was mentioning that he had friends who were Communists; his nickname for her: "Fonda-ling." When Jane first succumbed to his sexual advances, he yelled, "Hot dog!" She described him as a hyperactive Rhett Butler in need of Ritalin, a man who bought ranches faster than Fonda could apply makeup. The consummate narcissist, he banged his head against the wall when he perceived that his wife loved him as much as she loved Jesus. In her memoir, she wrote that Turner offered "Fountains-of-Versailles-and-fireworks sex." On the downside, he informed her that she should abandon her career because her last two movies were "real dogs." He added that the only negative in their relationship was her advanced age (the same as his own). The common denominator he shared with her former husband was a mental block against monogamy. After she discovered that he had taken a turn into infidelity in his office a month after their vows, she beat him on his shoulders with the car phone and poured bottled water on his head. Fonda moved into her daughter's house in Atlanta, even though that meant leaving a twenty-three-room palace.

In 2018, the eighty-one-year-old Fonda starred in *Book Club*, a geriatric version of *Sex and the City*, in which four senior ladies want to reinvigorate their sex lives after reading *Fifty Shades of Grey*. Fonda played a Samantha-like character, a leopard-skin-clad businesswoman, who scheduled sex devoid of commitment. The problem with producing the movie was that studio executives insisted on using actresses in their late forties. However, the creators persevered and found an independent company to finance the film. Jane declared that "ageism is alive and well" in the industry. Fonda's body is alluring as ever, and her face has escaped the ravages of time. She admitted to a facelift, undertaken because it "brought her ten extra years in the industry." The procedure probably did extend her screen time, as how many other eighty-year-old women have a hit comedy series on Netflix (*Grace and Frankie*), as well as a feature film, a documentary on her life about to air on HBO, and no indication of stopping any time soon? In her spare time, the lithe lady does yoga and Pilates and has made a new series of workout videos called "Prime Time," geared for older people. Jane admits she can no longer perform the fitness regime of yesteryear because of joint replacements. She says of the collateral damage of aging: "I have a fake hip, a fake knee, and I've had a number of back surgeries, so I'm sort of half-metal and half-bionic now. I have osteoarthritis and getting in and out of a car is a challenge. But I feel lucky that I did a lot of fitness work earlier in my life because it means I'm stronger now." Fonda entitled her memoir *My Life So Far*—a nod to her focus on the future—and wrote that her main form of exercise is jumping into things "before I really know what I'm doing. It's called a leap of faith. It's what keeps me young, too. That's my new workout."

Last year, she worked once more with Robert Redford, with whom she had starred in the 1967 film *Barefoot in the Park*. It centered on their fictional roles as intoxicated young newlyweds in New York who seldom left their bed. In the 2017 film, *Our Souls at Night*, they played widowed grandparents who get together to ward off the demons of loneliness. Although she had always harbored a romantic soft spot for Redford, she said, "I'm eighty. I've closed up shop down there." Her self-imposed celibacy indicated there would be no more *Fun with Dick and Jane*, to borrow the title of her 1977 film.

Despite Jane's three husbands and innumerable encounters of the close kind, in the end, her heart always belonged to her father. In 1981, she produced *On Golden Pond*—a story about an adult daughter trying to reconcile with her dad before his passing. Jane's hope was to get Henry the golden statuette that had always proved elusive. True to form, offstage, he would not discuss the emotional intimacy they shared on camera. When she needed succor during filming, she received it from costar Katherine Hepburn, who deemed Henry Fonda "cold, cold, cold." Jane collected the Oscar for Dad in what she called "the happiest moment of my life," and she delivered it to him at his home, as he was too ill to attend the ceremony. Sitting in his wheelchair, he did not say anything about it or offer a word of thanks. Life would have turned out far different for Jane if Henry Fonda had been Atticus Finch.

CHAPTER TWENTY-EIGHT

Order in the Court (1942)

The Old Testament praises the biblical king renowned for wisdom. His contemporary counterpart is a Queen Solomon, who dishes out justice and acerbic comments in equal measure, threatening to cut the baby in half to determine the real mother. As befits the times, the act is carried out from a television screen, not a throne, and publicists, rather than prophets, hail the diminutive septuagenarian.

In a nod to Fate—possessor of a vivid imagination—who would have guessed a Jewish girl from pre-women's-liberation Brooklyn would, in later life, become the doyenne of prime time? A star was born as Judith Susan Blum, daughter of Ethel, a homemaker, and Murray, a dentist, whom Judith described as "the greatest thing since sliced bread." She traced her sense of humor to her dad's dental practice, as, in the era before sedation, he distracted his patients by kibitzing and storytelling. Judy's lifelong best friend, Elaine Schwartz, recalled that Mrs. Blum "ran her husband's business, their lives, ran everything for the betterment of everything." Judith referred to her mother as "a meat and potato type of gal," the glue that held the family together. A serious student at the local James Madison High School, Judy loved to dance with her father to the sound of Sinatra LPs and bonded with her mother bargain-hunting at Loehmann's department store. David came along six years later, and the Blums vacationed at Catskills resorts where, Judy recalls, "My parents schlepped me around, so I would meet some nice rich guy." After all, for a girl of her background in the 1950s, the Holy Grail was an engagement ring. Possessed of an academic bent, she majored in government and attended New York Law School, the only female in a class of 126 students. By the time she graduated in 1965, she had wed attorney Ronald Levy. Her first job was as an attorney for a cosmetic firm; unhappy in the position, she quit and became a stay-at-home mother to Jamie and Adam. After moving to the suburbs, she felt stifled, and by 1972, Judy had returned to work. Mayor Ed Koch appointed her a family court judge, making her one of the first female judges in the country, and she presided over a Bronx family court. An endless parade appeared before her bench: battered infants, sexually abused minors, ugly custody battles, kids who raped at ten and murdered at eleven. Her trademark bluster came from prosecuting forty cases a day. Judy recalled, "I couldn't indulge people. It was like, 'You want a cathartic experience, get a shrink.'" Based on the low-wattage excuses Judy heard daily, she wrote *Don't Pee on My Leg and Tell Me It's Raining: America's Toughest Family Court Judge Speaks Out.* The title came from a comment she yelled at a teenage boy who claimed he began selling drugs after a death in his family. Her rejoinder, "Nobody goes out and sells crack because Grandma died. Get a better story!"

Four years later, Judy left her husband after twelve years of marriage. Her explanation for the marital breakdown: "We had different visions. He said, 'You work for fun, I work for a living.' It was a house full of friction and fighting over minutiae."

Three weeks after her divorce, Judy stopped in at Peggy Doyle's, a bar near the courts, where she met Jerry Sheindlin, a criminal defense lawyer. With her characteristic chutzpah, she "took one look, stuck my finger in his face and asked my girlfriend, 'Who's this?' Sometimes it just comes over you, an initial physical attraction, and that's what it was." Her two children and his three—Jerry had been separated from his wife Suzanne for four years—became an extended family. However, Judy was never Mrs. Brady from *The Brady Bunch.* When Adam asked for a hot lunch, his mother found a kosher pizzeria and gave him a slice with thumbtacks by telling him, "Stick this above the radiator. By noon you'll have a hot lunch." She informed her kids that, even if they wouldn't get tall from McDonald's, they wouldn't die from it either. Judge Judy was never cut out for the role of a chambermaid. After she proposed, the couple married a year later in the Library suite of the St. Regis Hotel. How did she "pop the question?" Judy said to Jerry, "Get out your datebook." What chance did Jerry have against Hurricane Judith?

At age seventy, when Murray died, grief from her father's passing eroded their marriage, and Judy once again became a divorcee. However, her ruling was not final. A year later, Judy called Elaine and told her to wash her face, as the couple were tying the knot once more within the hour. Judy's take on the traditional vow: "For better or forget it."

Judge Sheindlin had assumed that, after retirement, she would lead a quiet life in Florida, the typical destination for Jewish seniors. Mahjongg, bingo, and early-bird specials were no longer in the game plan when a 1993 *60 Minutes* episode captured her on camera. The audience ate up her signature tapping of her head while asking, "Does it say 'schmuck' here?" In her mid-fifties, while others are winding down, Sheindlin was ready to launch her second act.

Judge Judy premiered in 1996, a show on which the five-foot-one-inch, ninety-five-pound star of the bar sported a lace-trimmed judicial robe; its announcer opened each segment with the pronouncement, "Justice with an attitude." An example of this 'tude was when the judge told a nineteen-year-old man who did not seem to be exerting himself to support his children, "You made two babies. There have to be other parts of your body that work, sir." When two parties fought over the custody of a dog, Judge Sheindlin let the pooch run to the one it loved. Viewers adored the human polygraph whose mantra is that she has no time for stupid. The show catapulted her from New York family court judge to pop culture icon. America rose for the bench-mensch, and in its opening season, the show garnered the largest audience of any syndicated daytime program, crushing the competition from Oprah to Springer. The real-life small claims brought huge paydays that contrasted with her Manhattan judge salary of $113,000 per year. With her newfound wealth, in lieu of the West Coast condo, Judy owns five luxury homes, a Mercedes, and a private jet. She sold her yacht, *Triumphant Lady,* for $6.9 million. Sheindlin quips, regarding her many-splendored bank account, "We don't take Sweet 'n' Lows from restaurants anymore. I don't stuff dinner rolls into my pocketbook." However, some old habits never die, and she still eats her ritual Egg McMuffin, though now her chauffeur deposits her at the fast-food chain. Another tradition that has not changed is her iron discipline. Judy rises at 5:30 a.m., when she completes her twenty-minute workout in ten minutes. Her exercise routine is one of the reasons why she rocked a white bikini on her seventieth birthday, during a family vacation in the Bahamas.

The daytime doyenne's common theme, even when court has been adjourned, is to battle against what she calls "the dumbness of women who defer to men." Her argument is that husbands have a built-in helplessness, and the wives who enable them, unless they're Mother Teresa, will eventually explode. She remains mystified when women turn against one another to fight over an alcoholic man who has a chronic spot on the unemployment line. This philosophy led to her second book *Beauty Fades, Dumb is Forever: The Making of a Happy Woman.* Among her huge fan base was the novelist Kurt Vonnegut, who made the semi-serious suggestion that she should be a candidate to fill Justice Sandra Day O'Connor's seat on the country's highest bench. Despite Sheindlin's impatience with ignorance, a survey showed that ten percent of college students believe Judge Judy has a seat on the Supreme Court.

The queen bee of reality television has been on the air for twenty-one seasons and garners an average of ten million viewers per day. Her longevity with crime and punishment has paid off; her contract pays her a $47-million yearly salary that she negotiated till 2020. She supplemented this salary when she sold her show's archives to CBS for $95 million. Not too shabby a remuneration for informing defendants that "ummmm" is not a word and yelling at people in a fake court for their grammar and questionable life choices. Part of the appeal of the program is watching the scourge of the shiftless in action, an authentic robed avenger from the Justice League. Viewers find it satisfying to watch the less-than-stellar defendants get fricasseed; they are never adept at pulling the wool over the judge's eagle eye. Sheindlin met one of her fans when she attended a Shoah foundation dinner where President Obama was slated to win a humanitarian award. During the evening, she shook hands with the President. Asked by a nearby guest if he had ever watched her show, the Chief Executive responded, "Who doesn't love Judge Judy?"

Laurels have been planted on Sheindlin's brow topped with frosted, teased hair: In 1996, she received a star on the Hollywood Walk of Fame, in 2016 an Emmy, and in Season 9 of *Curb Your Enthusiasm*, Larry David stood before the formidable Judge Judy. In youth-obsessed TV, the seventy-five-year-old says she will only adjourn when the fun is gone and based on "How well my face is holding up." For her, retirement is something for other people.

Judith Sheindlin is a role model, and not because of her eye-popping income. Admiration stems from her entering law school when the legal field was a testosterone-dominated domain, and for donning a black robe rather than going quietly into a Florida sunset. In addition, transitioning from a Bronx courthouse to a Hollywood set took chutzpah. And, for those who are apprehensive that a career means tossing family on the altar of ambition, Judy proves this is not the case. Judith has remained in her long-term second/third marriage and is a fierce mother and grandmother to her

 dozen grandchildren. Another feather in her cap is that she

has not let age slow her down, and thus, she remains the long-running queen of reality television. And who knows what else lies under the sleeve of her judicial robe?

Sheindlin's take on why her show is a viewer-grabbing machine is, "I move swiftly, as opposed to a justice system that is slow and meandering." Her appeal is that she offers people a fantasy—a legal system as they would like it to be: fast and fair. Moreover, in a world steeped in chaos, with the septuagenarian wielding the gavel, Judge Judy maintains order in the court.

EPILOGUE

They Rock

The Lady Vanishes is not just the title of an Alfred Hitchcock movie; it describes the marginalization of women of a certain age. The sayings we have to describe the elderly reflect this mindset: long in the tooth, over the hill, past expiration date. The words hit close to home for females, conditioned by lifelong exposure to beauty magazines taking it as a given that desirability is the kissing cousin of beauty. As a result, we bid good riddance to our gray; we get pumped, lifted, and tucked; and we lie like hell when asked our age, which never hovers above forty, though, as children, we lived in terror of the Cold War. However, trying to look younger is analogous to a gay person masquerading as straight: It rarely fools anyone, and the effort is debilitating. Of course, the decades bring a host of physical ailments, and the situation is even more hurtful when younger people use the same voice with elders they do when speaking to kids, foreigners, or the feeble-minded. What I always found so painful was when strangers addressed me when speaking to my mother: how to make the elderly fifty shades of invisible. What the younger demographic does not understand is that inside an aging body is an individual who still has desires and dreams, something that dissipates when they are no longer seen, no longer heard. Dorothy Parker understood the hardship in navigating the terrain of age in her poem, "Afternoon," when she wrote, "I wish those blessed years / Were further than they be!"

On the upside, the years bring pluses; we want less, and we care less about what others think. Stepping off the hamster wheel in our farewell to youth is an important step in making the Golden Years, well, golden. After all, there is a tsunami of liberation in not giving a damn. What I have learned from researching the subjects profiled here is to embrace wrinkles, the roadmap of our past. To judge ourselves by the years on our birth certificates is testimony that the patriarchy has won: women wane in post-reproductive years. We must not succumb to the lie that we are more desirable, both to advertisers and partners, when in the eighteen-to-twenty-four age bracket. As teens, we burned our bras, at least figuratively, to protest sexism. Now, we must do the same, and set fire to our support hose to denounce ageism. The ladies burned the former to gain power; the latter, to hold onto it. Gerontophobia is the final frontier of discrimination.

The titles of Erica Jong's three books encapsulate the stages of the author's life: *Fear of Flying, Fear of Fifty, Fear of Dying.* The common denominator of the ladies in *Great Second Acts* is that they arm-wrestled age and were unstoppable till the end of their long lives. Many other women merited a chapter in *Great Second Acts*; for example, the legendary Joan Baez deserves to be recognized. Forever young at age seventy-seven in 2018, she went on a European tour and released an album, *Whistle Down the Wind.* In her role as singer/activist, she met some of the most iconic people of the twentieth century and was the lover of two famous men. An Australian journalist called her and asked, "Has it ever occurred to you that you are the only woman in the world to have seen both Steve Jobs and Bob Dylan naked?" to which Joan replied, "But not at the same time."

For allowing me to write a book in praise of older women, I have to thank my literary agent Roger Williams. The three-book deal he brokered has given me a purpose—the best antidote to aging. Brenda Knight has been my knight—always encouraging, always unstoppable. The last nod of gratitude is to my husband, Joel Geller, who always sees me through the lens of love, despite the ravages of Time. As Robert Browning wrote, "Grow old with me! The best is yet to be / The last of life, for which the first was made...." Love is the best Fountain of Youth.

By following in the footsteps of the women in *Great Second Acts*, we can thumb our noses at ageism, a phenomenon as old as time itself. Vintage wine, vintage cars, and vintage clothes are not the only hallmark of worth. The Roman philosopher Seneca wrote in the first century AD, "Senectus morbidus est," "Old age is a disease." Fast-forward to Mark Zuckerberg, who declared, "Young people are just smarter." The battle is real. But, as the women in my book prove, older ladies do not need rocking chairs. They rock.

Marlene Wagman-Geller
San Diego, California 2018

I would love to hear from you at onceagaintozelda@hotmail. com.

Lastly, when I have asked people to write reviews, they usually respond with the same look as if I had requested a vital organ. However, if the spirit moves, please leave one on Amazon / Goodreads.

"Warning"

By Jenny Joseph

When I am an old woman I shall wear purple
With a red hat which doesn't go, and doesn't suit me.
And I shall spend my pension on brandy and summer gloves
And satin sandals, and say we've no money for butter.
I shall sit down on the pavement when I'm tired
And gobble up samples in shops and press alarm bells
And run my stick along the public railings
And make up for the sobriety of my youth.
I shall go out in my slippers in the rain
And pick flowers in other people's gardens
And learn to spit.

You can wear terrible shirts and grow more fat
And eat three pounds of sausages at a go
Or only bread and pickle for a week
And hoard pens and pencils and beermats and things
in boxes.

But now we must have clothes that keep us dry
And pay our rent and not swear in the street
And set a good example for the children.
We must have friends to dinner and read the papers.

But maybe I ought to practice a little now?
So people who know me are not too shocked and surprised
When suddenly I am old, and start to wear purple.

Chapter 1—Anna Mary Robertson Moses

"Art: Presents from Grandma." *Time*, December 28, 1953. http:/content.time.com/time/magazine/article/0,9171,858436,00.html.

Cotter, Holland. "The Fenimore Art Museum Reconsiders an American Idol Named GrandmaMoses." *The New York Times*, August 4, 2006. https:/www.nytimes.com/2006/08/04/arts/design/04mose.html.

"Grandma Moses Is Dead at 101; Primitive Artist 'Just Wore Out.'" *The New York Times*, December 14, 1961. https:/archive.nytimes.com/www.nytimes.com/learning/general/onthisday/bday/0907.html.

Rhodes, Jesse. "Remembering Grandma Moses." *Smithsonian*, September 7, 2010. https:/www.smithsonianmag.com/smithsonian-institution/remembering-grandma-moses-622005/.

Schjeldahl, Peter. "Grandma Moses Looks Better Than Ever." *The New Yorker*, May 28, 2001. https:/www.newyorker.com/magazine/2001/05/28/the-original.

Waxman, Olivia B. "Grandma Moses Didn't Start Painting until Her 70s. Here's Why." *Time*, September 7, 2016. http:/time.com/4482257/grandma-moses-history/.

Chapter 2—Loretta Mary Aiken/Jackie "Moms" Mabley"

Benedictus, Leo. "Comedy Gold: Jackie 'Moms' Mabley." *The Guardian*, November 14, 2013. https:/www.theguardian.com/stage/2013/nov/14/comedy-gold-jackie-moms-mabley-compilation.

Bennetts, Leslie. "Theater; The Pain behind the Laughter of Moms Mabley." *The New York Times*, August 9, 1987. https://www.nytimes.com/1987/08/09/theater/theater-the-pain-behind-the-laughter-of-moms-mabley.html.

McDonald, Soraya Nadia. "Moms Mabley: No Patience for Respectability Politics." *The Washington Post*, November 24, 2013. https://www.washingtonpost.com/blogs/she-the-people/wp/2013/11/24/moms-mabley-no-patience-for-respectability-politics/.

Mondello, Bob. "Moms Dearest." *Washington City Paper*, January 5, 1996. https://www.washingtoncitypaper.com/arts/theater/article/13009943/moms-dearest.

Murphy, Mekado. "The Comedy Pioneer in the Floppy Hat." *The New York Times*, November 15, 2013. https://www.nytimes.com/2013/11/17/arts/television/whoopi-goldbergs-documentary-on-moms-mabley.html.

Muther, Christopher. "An Overdue Look at the Comedy of Moms Mabley." *The Boston Globe*, November 18, 2013. https://www.bostonglobe.com/arts/television/2013/11/18/goldberg-offers-overdue-look-comedy-moms-mabley-hbo-documentary/8vOeYJSjOThBlH96RSLSJM/story.html.

New York Times Staff. "Moms Mabley, 77 Comedienne of TV, Stage, and Radio, Dead." *The New York Times*, May 24, 1975. https://www.nytimes.com/1975/05/24/archives/moms-mabley-77-comedienne-of-tv-stage-and-radio-dead.html.

Nussbaum, Emily. "Below the Belt." *The New Yorker*, November 25, 2013.https://www.newyorker.com/magazine/2013/11/25/below-the-belt.

Simmons, Shanell. "Moms Mabley Honored by HBO." *Ebony*, November 12, 2013.https://www.ebony.com/entertainment-culture/moms-mabley-honored-by-hbo-888.

Chapter 3—Golda Meir

Herrmann, Dorothy. "Irresistible Golda: The Life-and Loves-of Israel's Golda Meir." *Chicago Tribune*, December 11, 1988. http:/articles.chicagotribune.com/1988-12-11/entertainment/8802240220_1_golda-meir-arab-attacks-minister.

Peres, Shimon. "Theater; Always a Lioness, Protecting Her Beloved Israel." *The New York Times*, March 16, 2003. http://www.nytimes.com/2003/03/16/theater/theater-always-a-lioness-protecting-her-beloved-israel.html.

Shlaim, Avi. "The Face That Launched a Thousand MiGs." *The Guardian*, August 15, 2008. https:/www.theguardian.com/books/2008/aug/16/biography.politics.

Chapter 4— Beatrice Wood

Beatrice Wood Center for the Arts. "About Beatrice Wood." http:/www.beatricewood.com/biography.html.

"Ceramist, 'Mama of Dada' Beatrice Wood Dies at 105." *The Washington Post*, March 15, 1998. https:/www.washingtonpost.com/archive/local/1998/03/15/ceramist-mama-of-dada-beatrice-wood-dies-at-105/958c2ea1-4720-4a53-8354-f5cbfbaf30f8/.

Cooper, Emmanuel. "Obituary: Beatrice Wood." *The Independent*, March 19, 1998. https://www.independent.co.uk/news/obituaries/obituary-beatrice-wood-1151106.html.

Curtis, Karen. "The 'Real' Rose Calvert from *Titanic*." *Reel Rundown*, September 7, 2017. https:/reelrundown.com/film-industry/Beatrice-Wood-The-Woman-James-Cameron-Modeled-Rose-Calvert-in-Titanic-After.

Haithman, Diane. "Ceramist Beatrice Wood, the 'Mama of Dada,' Dies." *Los Angeles Times*, March 13, 1998. http:/articles.latimes.com/1998/mar/13/news/mn-28425.

Kimmelman, Michael. "The Lives They Lived: Beatrice Wood; A 'Titanic' Figure of the Avant-Garde." *The New York Times Magazine*, January 3, 1999. https:/www.nytimes.com/1999/01/03/magazine/the-lives-they-lived-beatrice-wood-a-titanic-figure-of-the-avant-garde.html.

Rusoff, Jane Wollman. "Her Heart Belongs to Dada." *The Washington Post*, March 3, 1993. https:/www.washingtonpost.com/archive/lifestyle/1993/03/03/her-heart-belongs-to-dada/bd55e465-53fd-468d-8458-3af60ab78f78/.

Smith, Roberta. "Beatrice Wood, 105, Potter and Mama of Dada, Is Dead." *The New York Times*, March 14, 1998. https:/www.nytimes.com/1998/03/14/arts/beatrice-wood-105-potter-and-mama-of-dada-is-dead.html.

Chapter 5—Ruth Gordon Jones

Freedman, Samuel G. "Ruth Gordon, The Actress, Dies At 88." *The New York Times*, August 29, 1985. https:/www.nytimes.com/1985/08/29/arts/ruth-gordon-the-actress-dies-at-88.html.

Gussow, Mel. "Stage View; Grit and Wit Made Ruth Gordon a Star." *The New York Times*, September 8,1985. https:/www.nytimes.com/1985/09/08/arts/stage-view-grit-and-wit-made-ruth-gordon-a-star.html.

Houseman, John. "My Side." *The New York Times*, October 10, 1976. https:/www.nytimes.com/1976/10/10/archives/my-side-life-with-lindsay-and-crouse-life-with.html.

Pearson, Richard. "Renowned Actress Ruth Gordon Dies." *The Washington Post*, August 29, 1985. https:/www. washingtonpost.com/archive/local/1985/08/29/renowned-actress-ruth-gordon-dies/2ec86b7f-14dd-4057-b0bb-8d76c83fd962/.

Wada, Karen. "Ruth Gordon Dies; Stage, Film Career Spanned 7 Decades." *Los Angeles Times*, August 29, 1985. http:/articles.latimes.com/1985-08-29/news/mn-23770_1_ruth-gordon

Chapter 6— Margaret Kuhn

"Activist, in 70's, Says Age Distinguishes Her." *The New York Times*, March 12, 1984. http:/www.nytimes.com/1984/03/12/us/activist-in-70-s-says-age-distinguishes-her.html.

Folkart, Burt A. "Maggie Kuhn, 89; Iconoclastic Founder of Gray Panthers." *Los Angeles Times*, April 23, 1995. http:/articles.latimes.com/1995-04-23/news/mn-58042_1_maggie-kuhn.

Hostetler, A. J. "Maggie Kuhn, 86, Still Stirs Consciousness: Gray Panthers: She Is Proud of Her Involvement in Civil Rights, Peace, Labor, Environmental Movements." *Los Angeles Times*, March 8, 1992. http:/articles.latimes.com/1992-03-08/news/mn-6325_1_gray-panthers.

Levy, Claudia. "Gray Panthers Co-Founder Maggie Kuhn Dies at 89." *The Washington Post*, April 23, 1995. https:/www.washingtonpost.com/archive/local/1995/04/23/gray-panthers-co-founder-maggie-kuhn-dies-at-89/a7c55189-b388-4e95-aafe-0d7d9a9163a1/.

Thomas, Robert McG., Jr. "Maggie Kuhn, 89, the Founder of the Gray Panthers, Is Dead." *The New York Times*, April 23, 1995. http:/www.nytimes.com/1995/04/23/obituaries/maggie-kuhn-89-the-founder-of-the-gray-panthers-is-dead.html.

Wahl, Timothy. "Remembering Maggie Kuhn, Firebrand of the Aged." *The Epoch Times*, December 1, 2016. https:/www.theepochtimes.com/remembering-maggie-kuhn-firebrand-of-the-aged_2193282.html.

Williams, Jasmin K. "Maggie Kuhn and the Gray Panthers." *New York Post*, March 21, 2005. https:/nypost.com/2005/03/21/maggie-kuhn-and-the-gray-panthers/.

Chapter 7—Rita Levi-Montalcini

Carey, Benedict. "Dr. Rita Levi-Montalcini, Nobel Winner, Dies at 103." *The New York Times*, December 30, 2012. https:/www.nytimes.com/2012/12/31/science/dr-rita-levi-montalcini-a-revolutionary-in-the-study-of-the-brain-dies-at-103.html.

Costandi, Mo. "Obituary: Rita Levi-Montalcini." *The Guardian*, January 1, 2013. https:/www.theguardian.com/science/neurophilosophy/2013/jan/01/rita-levi-montalcini-obituary.

Langer, Emily. "Rita Levi-Montalcini, Nobel Prize-winning Neuroscientist, Dies at 103." The Washington Post, December 30, 2012. https:/www.washingtonpost.com/national/health-science/rita-levi-montalcini-nobel-prize-winning-neuroscientist-dies-at-103/2012/12/30/054829e0-5295-11e2-a613-ec8d394535c6_story.html.

McElheny, Victor K. "A Self-Made Scientist." *The New York Times*, 1988. https:/www.nytimes.com/1988/05/01/books/a-self-made-scientist.html.

Popham, Peter. "Is This the Secret of Eternal Life?" *The Independent*, April 25, 2009. https:/www.independent.co.uk/news/science/is-this-the-secret-of-eternal-life-1674005.html.

"Rita Levi-Montalcini." *The Telegraph*, December 31, 2012. https:/www.telegraph.co.uk/news/obituaries/9773327/Rita-Levi-Montalcini.html.

"Rita Levi-Montalcini, Biologist, Died on December 30th, Aged 103." *The Economist*, January 5, 2013. https:/www.economist.com/obituary/2013/01/05/rita-levi-montalcini.

Tucker, Anthony. "Rita Levi-Montalcini Obituary." *The Guardian*, December 30, 2012. https:/www.theguardian.com/science/2012/dec/30/rita-levi-montalcini.

Chapter 8— Mother Teresa

Kaufman, Michael T. "The World of Mother Teresa; Mother Teresa." *The New York Times*, December 9, 1979. https:/www.nytimes.com/1979/12/09/archives/the-world-of-mother-teresa-mother-teresa.html.

Kenny, Mary. "Obituary: Mother Teresa of Calcutta." The Independent, September 6, 1997. https:/www.independent.co.uk/news/obituaries/obituary-mother-teresa-of-calcutta-1237661.html.

"Mother Teresa." The Telegraph, September 6, 1997. https:/www.telegraph.co.uk/news/obituaries/5872071/Mother-Teresa.html.

Pace, Eric. "Mother Teresa, Hope of the Despairing, Dies at 87." The New York Times, September 6, 1997. https:/www.nytimes.com/1997/09/06/world/mother-teresa-hope-of-the-despairing-dies-at-87.html.

Bergan, Ronald. "Marta Eggerth Obituary." *The Guardian*, December 30, 2013. https:/www.theguardian.com/ film/2013/dec/30/marta-eggerth.

Fawkes, Richard. "Marta Eggerth: Star of Light Opera Regarded as the Definitive 'Merry Widow' Who Inspired Film and Stage Directors Alike." *The Independent*, January 1, 2014. https:/www.independent.co.uk/news/obituaries/ marta-eggerth-star-of-light-opera-regarded-as-the-definitive-merry-widow-who-inspired-film-and-stage-9032044.html.

Fox, Margalit. "Marta Eggerth, the 'Callas of Operetta,' Dies at 101." *The New York Times*, December 30, 2013. https:/www. nytimes.com/2013/12/31/arts/music/marta-eggerth-the-callas-of-operetta-dies-at-101.html.

"Marta Eggerth." *The Times*, January 1, 2014. https:/www. thetimes.co.uk/article/marta-eggerth-j3qv75Oz7l2.

"Márta Eggerth – Obituary." *The Telegraph*, December 29, 2013. https:/www.telegraph.co.uk/news/obituaries/10541544/ Marta-Eggerth-obituary.html.

Midgette, Anne. "Marta Eggerth, Still Singing at 100." *The Washington Post*, April 11, 2012. https:/www. washingtonpost.com/entertainment/music/marta-eggerth-still-singing-at-100/2012/04/11/glQAZgzXBT_ story.html.

"Marta Eggerth, 101; Was Famed Singer and Actress." *The Washington Post*, January 1, 2014. https:/www. bostonglobe.com/metro/obituaries/2013/12/31/ marta-eggerth-operetta-singer-and-film-star-dies/ JY6ROFpnVBH37nQo1gAe9K/story.html.

Adams, Richard. "Dorothy Height, 'Godmother of the Civil
    Rights Movement'." *The Guardian*, April 20, 2010.
    https:/www.theguardian.com/world/richard-adams-
    blog/2010/apr/20/dorothy-height-civil-rights-pioneer.

Barnes, Bart. "Dorothy I. Height, Founding Matriarch of U.S.
    Civil Rights Movement, Dies at 98." *The Washington Post*,
    April 21, 2010. http:/www.washingtonpost.com/wp-dyn/
    content/article/2010/04/20/AR2010042001287.html.

Diliberto, Gioia. "She Shall Overcome." *The New York Times*,
    October 5, 2003. https:/www.nytimes.com/2003/10/05/
    books/she-shall-overcome.html.

"Dorothy Height." *The Telegraph*, April 21, 2010. https:/www.
    telegraph.co.uk/news/obituaries/7615645/Dorothy-
    Height.html.

Fox, Margalit. "Dorothy Height, Largely Unsung Giant of the
    Civil Rights Era, Dies at 98." *The New York Times*, April 20,
    2010. https:/www.nytimes.com/2010/04/21/us/21height.
    html.

Height, Dorothy. *Open Wide the Freedom Gates: A Memoir*. New
    York: PublicAffairs, 2005.

Hodgson, Godfrey. "Dorothy Height Obituary." *The Guardian*,
    April 25, 2010. https:/www.theguardian.com/
    theguardian/2010/apr/25/dorothy-height-obituary.

Stewart, Jocelyn. "Dorothy Height Dies at 98; Key Figure in the
    Civil Rights Movement." *Los Angeles Times*, April 20, 2010.
    http:/www.latimes.com/local/la-me-dorothy-height-
    20100420-story.html.

"Mary Kay Ash." *The Telegraph*, December 5, 2001. https://www.telegraph.co.uk/news/obituaries/1364324/Mary-Kay-Ash.html.

"Mary Kay Ash Dies." *The Washington Post*, November 23, 2001. https://www.washingtonpost.com/archive/local/2001/11/23/mary-kay-ash-dies/1755b79f-5947-484f-b10c-db3a22b82ab1/.

McMurran, Kristin. "Mary Kay Ash." *People*, July 29, 1985.https://people.com/archive/mary-kay-ash-vol-24-no-5/.

Nemy, Enid. "Mary Kay Ash Who Built a Cosmetics Empire and Adored Pink is Dead at 83." *The New York Times*, November 23, 2001. https://www.nytimes.com/2001/11/23/business/mary-kay-ash-who-built-a-cosmetics-empire-and-adored-pink-is-dead-at-83.html.

Wagman-Geller, Marlene. *Eureka! The Surprising Stories that Changed the World*. New York: TarcherPerigee, 2010.

Chapter 12—Tao Porchon-Lynch

Abrams, Margaret. "A 98-Year-Old Yoga Master Reveals Her Mantra." *Observer*, January 12, 2017. http://observer.com/2017/01/oldest-yogi-tao-porchon-lynch-advice/.

Davies, Madeleine. "98-Year-Old 'Yogalebrity' Täo Porchon-Lynch Never Drinks Water, But Sure Loves Her Wine." *Jezebel*, November 28, 2016. https://jezebel.com/98-year-old-yogalebrity-tao-porchon-lynch-never-drinks-1789429576.

Feng, Cathy Hilborn. "A 99-year-old Yoga Teacher's Amazing Life and Youthful Spirit, and the People She's Known, from Gandhi to Marlene Dietrich." *South China Morning Post*, December 27, 2017. http:/www.scmp.com/lifestyle/health-beauty/article/2125669/99-year-old-yoga-teachers-amazing-life-and-youthful-spirit.

Gregoire, Carolyn. "Tao Porchon-Lynch, 94-Year-Old Yogi, Shares Secrets to Health & Longevity." *HuffPost*, May 8, 2013. https:/www.huffingtonpost.com/2013/05/08/tao-porchon-lynch_n_3209187.html.

Live, Herald. "Tao, 98-year-old Poster Child for Yoga and Wellness." *Africa News Hub*, January 30, 2017. https:/www.africanewshub.com/news/6284110-tao-98-year-old-poster-child-for-yoga-and-wellness.

Newsweek Special Edition. "An Ageless Spirit—Yogi Still Teaching at 98." *Newsweek*, August 28, 2016. http:/www.newsweek.com/ageless-spirit-tao-still-teaching-yoga-98-ageless-spirit-tao-still-teaching-493522.

Rosman, Katherine. "A 98-Year-Old Yoga Celebrity Tells All." *The New York Times*, November 26, 2016. https:/www.nytimes.com/2016/11/26/fashion/tao-porchon-lynch-oldest-living-yoga-celebrity.html.

—. "98 and Dancing: On Her Third Artificial Hip, a Post Child for the Active Life." *The Herald Tribune*, December 20, 2016. http:/www.heraldtribune.com/news/20161220/98-and-dancing-on-her-third-artificial-hip-poster-child-for-active-life.

Chapter 13— Leah Chase

Allen, Carol. *Leah Chase: Listen, I Say Like This*. Gretna: Pelican Publishing Company, 2002.

Anderson, Brett. "New Orleans's Queen of Creole Cooking, at Ninety-Three." *The New Yorker*, April 13, 2016. https://www.newyorker.com/culture/culture-desk/new-orleanss-queen-of-creole-cooking-at-ninety-three.

Jenkins, Nancy Harmon. "Cooks on the Map - This Month: Leah Chase, New Orleans; A Lover of Food Who Nurtured a New Orleans Institution." *The New York Times*, June 27, 1990. https://www.nytimes.com/1990/06/27/garden/cooks-map-this-month-leah-chase-new-orleans-lover-food-who-nurtured-new-orleans.html.

McNulty, Ian. "The Extraordinary Life of Leah Chase - Ian McNulty on New Orleans' Queen of Creole Cuisine." *Gambit Weekly*, May 22, 2012. https://www.theadvocate.com/gambit/new_orleans/news/article_53717e22-de30-506b-86d2-278486800ce4.html.

"91-year-old 'Queen of Creole Cuisine' Pours Faith into Cooking." Loyola Press. https://www.loyolapress.com/our-catholic-faith/prayer/arts-and-faith/culinary-arts/91-year-old-queen-of-creole-cuisine.

Severson, Kim. "In New Orleans, Knives, Forks and Hammers." *The New York Times*, August 23, 2006. https://www.nytimes.com/2006/08/23/dining/23orleans.html.

Stroup, Sheila. "Chef Leah Chase Still Warming up Her Kitchen at 92." *The Times-Picayune*, January 10, 2015. http://www.nola.com/dining/index.ssf/2015/01/chef_leah_chase_still_warming.html.

Chapter 14— Judith Jones

"Editor Who Published Julia Child and Anne Frank's Diary." *The Irish Times*, August 12, 2017. https://www.irishtimes.com/life-and-style/people/editor-who-published-julia-child-and-anne-frank-s-diary-1.3182620.

Italie, Hillel. "Judith Jones, Editor of Julia Child's First
   Cookbook, Dead at 93." *The Globe and Mail*, August 2, 2017.
   https:/www.theglobeandmail.com/arts/books-and-
   media/judith-jones-editor-of-julia-child-dead-at-93/
   article35862844/.

McFadden, Robert D. "Editor of Literature and Culinary
   Delight, Dies at 93." *The New York Times*, August 2, 2017.
   https:/www.nytimes.com/2017/08/02/us/judith-jones-
   dead.html.

Severson, Kim. "Remembering Judith Jones and Her Recipe
   for Food Writing." *The New York Times*, August 2, 2017.
   https:/www.nytimes.com/2017/08/02/dining/judith-
   jones-food-editor.html.

Yonan, Joe. "Judith Jones, Cookbook Editor Who Brought Julia
   Child and Others to the Table, Dies at 93." *The Washington
   Post*, August 2, 2017. https:/www.washingtonpost.com/
   local/obituaries/judith-jones-cookbook-author-who-
   brought-julia-child-and-others-to-the-table-dies-at-
   93/2017/08/02/611b527c-7781-11e7-8f39-eeb7d3a2d304_
   story.html.

Chapter 15— Helen Bamber

Bernstein, Adam. "Helen Bamber, Who Helped War,
   Genocide and Torture Victims Recover, Dies at 89."
   The Washington Post, August 26, 2014. https:/www.
   washingtonpost.com/world/helen-bamber-who-
   helped-war-genocide-and-torture-victims-recover-
   dies-at-89/2014/08/26/23cc1eac-2c6a-11e4-994d-
   202962a9150c_story.html.

Birdi, T.J. "Helen Bamber Obituary." *The Guardian*, August 24,
   2014. https:/www.theguardian.com/law/2014/aug/24/
   helen-bamber.

Martin, Douglas. "Helen Bamber, Therapist to Torture Victims, Dies at 89." *The New York Times,* August 27, 2014. https:/www.nytimes.com/2014/08/28/world/helen-bamber-therapist-to-torture-victims-dies-at-89.html.

Selby, Jenn. "Helen Bamber Dies: Human Rights Campaigner Who Worked with Survivors of the Nazi Holocaust Was 89." *The Independent,* August 22, 2014. http:/www.independent.co.uk/news/people/helen-bamber-dies-human-rights-campaigner-who-worked-with-survivors-of-the-nazi-holocaust-passes-9685043.html.

"Small Wonder." *The Guardian,* March 10, 2000. https:/www.theguardian.com/politics/2000/mar/11/women.

Chapter 16—Simone Veil

Associated Press. "Simone Veil, iconic European feminist politician, dies at 89." *Los Angeles Times,* June 30, 2017. http:/www.latimes.com/local/obituaries/la-fg-simone-veil-obituary-20170630-story.html.

Badinter, Robert. "Simone Veil Remembered." *The Guardian,* December 17, 2017. https:/www.theguardian.com/world/2017/dec/17/simone-veil-remembered-by-robert-badinter.

Breeden, Aurelien. "Simone Veil to Be Laid to Rest in Panthéon, among France's Revered." *The New York Times,* July 5, 2017. https:/www.nytimes.com/2017/07/05/world/europe/simone-veil-pantheon.html.

Chan, Sewell. "Simone Veil, Ex-Minister Who Wrote France's Abortion Law, Dies at 89." *The New York Times,* June 30, 3017. https:/www.nytimes.com/2017/06/30/world/europe/simone-veil-dead.html.

"Holocaust Survivor Who Became Champion of France's Abortion Law." *The Irish Times*, July 8, 2017. https:/ www.irishtimes.com/life-and-style/people/holocaust-survivor-who-became-champion-of-france-s-abortion-law-1.3146766.

Langer, Emily. "Simone Veil, French Holocaust Survivor and Statesman, Dies at 89." *The Washington Post*, June 30, 2017. https:/www.washingtonpost.com/local/obituaries/simone-veil-french-holocaust-survivor-and-statesman-dies-at-89/2017/06/30/83ebe7b8-5d9a-11e7-a9f6-7c3296387341_story.html.

"Simone Veil Obituary: Holocaust Survivor and Statesman Who Fought for Abortion Rights." *The Independent*, July 4, 2017. https:/www.independent.co.uk/news/obituaries/simone-veil-obituary-france-holocaust-survivor-abortion-rights-paris-a7820831.html.

Our Foreign Staff. "Simone Veil Dies at 89: The Legacy of the French Auschwitz Survivor and Women's Rights Icon." *The Telegraph*, June 30, 2017. https:/www.telegraph.co.uk/news/2017/06/30/simone-veil-dies-89-legacy-french-auschwitz-survivor-womens/.

Poirier, Agnès. "Farewell Simone Veil, Conscience of France." *The Guardian*, July 8, 2017. https:/www.theguardian.com/commentisfree/2017/jul/09/farewell-simone-veil-conscience-of-france.

Wadham, Lucy. "France's Real First Lady." *New Statesman*, April 9, 2009. https:/www.newstatesman.com/books/2009/04/simone-veil-life-france-woman.

Associated Press. "Shirley Temple Black, Beloved Child Actress, Won Praise in Diplomatic Career." Daily News, February 11, 2014. http://www.nydailynews.com/news/politics/shirley-temple-won-praise-diplomatic-career-article-1.1609333.

Bergan, Ronald. "Shirley Temple Black Obituary." *The Guardian*, February 11, 2014. https:/www.theguardian.com/film/2014/feb/11/shirley-temple-black.

Harmetz, Aljean. "Shirley Temple Black, Hollywood's Biggest Little Star, Dies at 85." *The New York Times*, February 11, 2014. https:/www.nytimes.com/2014/02/12/arts/shirley-temple-black-screen-star-dies-at-85.html.

Marinucci, Carla. "Shirley Temple Black Excelled in 2nd Career in Diplomacy." *SFGate*, February 12, 2014. https:/www.sfgate.com/politics/article/Shirley-Temple-Black-excelled-in-2nd-career-in-5226086.php.

McMurran, Kristin. "Shirley Temple Black Taps Out a Telling Memoir of Child Stardom." *People*, November 28, 1988. http:/people.com/archive/shirley-temple-black-taps-out-a-telling-memoir-of-child-stardom-vol-30-no-22/.

Reuters. "Shirley Temple Black, Former Hollywood Child Star, Dies at 85." *Newsweek*, February 11, 2014. http:/www.newsweek.com/shirley-temple-black-former-hollywood-child-star-dies-85-228718/.

"Shirley Temple Black, Actress and Diplomat, Died on February 10th, aged 85." *The Economist*, February 15, 2014. https:/www.economist.com/news/obituary/21596495-shirley-temple-black-actress-and-diplomat-died-february-10th-aged-85-shirley-temple.

Smith, Kyle. "Picture Perfect." *People*, June 8, 1998. http:/people.com/archive/picture-perfect-vol-49-no-22/.

Verger, Rob. "Newsweek Rewind: When We Reported on Shirley Temple Black." *Newsweek,* February 12, 2014. http:/www.newsweek.com/newsweek-rewind-when-we-reported-shirley-temple-black-228859.

Chapter 18— China Machado

Domonoske, Camila. "China Machado, Groundbreaking Model, Muse and Editor, Dies at 86." *NPR,* December 20, 2016. https:/www.npr.org/sections/thetwoway/2016/12/20/506289814/ china-machado-groundbreaking-model-muse-and-editor-dies-at-86.

Friedman, Vanessa. "China Machado, Breakthrough Model Until the End, Dies at 86." *The New York Times,* December 19, 2016. https:/www.nytimes.com/2016/12/19/fashion/china-machado-first-non-white-supermodel.html.

Mulkerrins, Jane. "China Machado on Her Fabulous Life." *The Telegraph,* March 5, 2013. http:/fashion.telegraph.co.uk/news-features/TMG9899911/China-Machado-on-her-fabulous-life.html.

Okwodu, Janelle. "Remembering China Machado, Supermodel and Fashion Influencer." *Vogue,* December 18, 2016. https:/www.vogue.com/article/china-machado-model-tribute.

Owens, Mitchell. "Fine China." *The New York Times Magazine,* August 18, 2002. https:/www.nytimes.com/2002/08/18/magazine/fine-china.html.

Wilkinson, Isabel . "China Machado in 'About Face': A Fashion Legend Takes on Aging." *The Daily Beast,* July 30, 2012. https:/www.thedailybeast.com/china-machado-in-about-face-a-fashion-legend-takes-on-aging.

Yuan, Jada. "I Didn't Think of Myself as Good-Looking at All." *New York,* August 14, 2011. http:/nymag.com/fashion/11/fall/china-machado/.

Chen, Joyce. "Edith Windsor, Same-Sex Marriage Activist, Dead at 88." *Rolling Stone*, September 12, 2017. https:/ www.rollingstone.com/culture/news/edith-windsor-same-sex-marriage-lgbt-activist-dead-at-88-w502700.

Gabbatt, Adam. "Edith Windsor and Thea Spyer: 'A Love Affair that Just Kept on and on and on.'" *The Guardian*, June 26, 2013. https:/www.theguardian.com/world/2013/jun/26/edith-windsor-thea-spyer-doma.

Gray, Eliza. "Edith Windsor, The Unlikely Activist." *Time*, December 11, 2013. http:/poy.time.com/2013/12/11/runner-up-edith-windsor-the-unlikely-activist/.

Langer, Emily. "Edith Windsor, Who Led Fight for Federal Benefits for Same-sex Couples, Dies at 88." *The Washington Post*, September 13, 2017. https:/www.washingtonpost.com/local/obituaries/edith-windsor-who-led-fight-for-federal-benefits-for-same-sex-couples-dies-at-88/2017/09/13/c4b6452a-988e-11e7-82e4-f1076f6d6152_story.html.

Levy, Ariel. "Postscript: Edith Windsor, 1929-2017." *The New Yorker*, September 14, 2017. https:/www.newyorker.com/news/news-desk/postscript-edith-windsor-1929-2017.

Redden, Molly. "Edith Windsor, Icon of Gay Rights Movement, Dies Aged 88." *The Guardian*, September 13, 2017. https:/www.theguardian.com/us-news/2017/sep/12/edith-windsor-lgbt-rights-activist-dies-at-88.

Socarides, Richard. "The Legacy of Edith Windsor." *The New Yorker*, September 13, 2017. https:/www.newyorker.com/news/daily-comment/the-legacy-of-edith-windsor.

Thrasher, Steven W. "Goodbye, Edie Windsor. Thank You for Never Giving up." *The Guardian*, September 13, 2017. https://www.theguardian.com/commentisfree/2017/sep/13/edith-windsor-lgbt-tribute.

Chapter 20— Dolores Huerta

Clarke, Cath. "Dolores Review – Powerful Portrait of Mexican-American Activist." *The Guardian*,

December 1, 2017. https://www.theguardian.com/film/2017/dec/01/dolores-review-feminist-dolores-huerta-yes-we-can-peter-bratt-documentary.

Felsenthal, Julia. "At 87, Dolores Huerta Is Finally Getting Her Due." *Vogue*, September 1, 2017. https://www.vogue.com/article/dolores-huerta-documentary.

Grady, Pam. "UFW co-founder Dolores Huerta champions new causes today." *San Francisco Chronicle*, April 7, 2017. https://www.sfchronicle.com/movies/article/UFW-co-founder-Dolores-Huerta-champions-new-11058505.php.

Jaworowski, Ken. "Review: Workers Have a Friend in the Determined 'Dolores'." *The New York Times*, August 31, 2017. https://www.nytimes.com/2017/08/31/movies/dolores-review.html.

Merry, Stephanie. "The New Documentary 'Dolores' has a Few Lessons for the #resistance." *The Washington Post*, September 13, 2017. https://www.washingtonpost.com/news/arts-and-entertainment/wp/2017/09/13/the-new-documentary-dolores-has-a-few-lessons-for-the-resistance/.

Philp, Drew. "'Yes, We Can': Dolores Huerta, Architect of Slogan, Gets the Spotlight in New Film." *The Guardian*, November 30, 2017. https://www.theguardian.com/us-news/2017/nov/30/dolores-huerta-yes-we-can.

Quiñones, Michael. "Dolores Director Takes Us Behind the Scenes of His Acclaimed Film on Labor and Feminist Activist Dolores Huerta." *People*, March 27, 2018. http:// people.com/chica/activist-dolores-huerta-documentary-debuts-on-pbs/.

Smith, Ryan P. "Civil Rights Icon Dolores Huerta Offers Advice to a New Generation of Activists." *Smithsonian*, August 25, 2017. https:/www.smithsonianmag.com/smithsonian-institution/civil-rights-icon-dolores-huerta-offers-advise-new-generation-activists-180964630/.

Chapter 22— Rita Moreno

Cahalan, Susannah. "Rita Moreno Tells All about Her 'Near-Fatal' Affair with Marlon Brando in Memoir." *New York Post*, February 17, 2013. https:/nypost.com/2013/02/17/ rita-moreno-tells-all-about-her-near-fatal-affair-with-marlon-brando-in-memoir/.

Gates, Anita. "Center Stage: 'Rita Moreno: A Memoir.'" *The New York Times*, May 31, 2013. http:/www.nytimes. com/2013/06/02/books/review/rita-moreno-a-memoir. html.

Kaufman, Sarah. "Rita Moreno on Strength, Stamina and the Power of a Killer Body." *The Washington Post*, July 10, 2014. https:/www.washingtonpost.com/entertainment/ theater_dance/rita-moreno-on-strength-stamina-and-the-power-of-a-killer-body/2014/07/10/5882a6a6-0858-11e4-8a6a-19355c7e870a_story.html.

McElwaine, Sandra. "Rita Moreno, SAG Life Achievement Award Winner, Talks Brando, Elvis, and *West Side Story*." *The Daily Beast*, January 15, 2014. https:/www. thedailybeast.com/rita-moreno-sag-life-achievement-award-winner-talks-brando-elvis-and-west-side-story.

"Rita Moreno's Memoir is Survivor's Story." *Malta Independent*, April 30, 2013. http:/www.independent.com.mt/ articles/2013-04-30/books/Rita-Moreno's-memoir-is-survivor's-story-1495760896.

Chapter 21—Sister Megan Rice

Berrigan, Frida. "How a Nun, a Vet, and a Housepainter Stood Up to the Threat of Nuclear Weapons." *The Nation*, August 31, 2016. https:/www.thenation.com/article/how-a-nun-a-vet-and-a-housepainter-stood-up-to-the-threat-of-nuclear-weapons/.

Broad, William J. "The Nun Who Broke into the Nuclear Sanctum." *The New York Times*, August 10, 2012. https:/www.nytimes.com/2012/08/11/science/behind-nuclear-breach-a-nuns-bold-fervor.html.

"Sister Megan Rice, Freed from Prison, Looks ahead to More Anti-Nuclear Activism." *The New York Times*, May 26, 2015. https:/www.nytimes.com/2015/05/27/science/sister-megan-rice-anti-nuclear-weapons-activist-freed-from-prison.html.

Crocker, Lizzie. "The Nuclear Nun Goes to Jail." *The Daily Beast*, February 18, 2014. https:/www.thedailybeast.com/the-nuclear-nun-goes-to-jail.

Hackman, Rose. "Sister Megan Rice: The 85-Year-Old Nun with a Criminal Record Remains Defiant." *The Guardian*, July 16, 2015. https:/www.theguardian.com/world/2015/jul/16/sister-megan-rice-nun-prison-nuclear-weapons-protest.

Hattenstone, Simon. "Star Trek's Nichelle Nichols: 'Martin Luther King was a Trekker.'" *The Guardian*, October 18, 2016. https:/www.theguardian.com/tv-and-radio/2016/oct/18/star-trek-nichelle-nichols-martin-luther-king-trekker.

Lloyd, Robert. "Television Review: 'Pioneers of Television.'" *Los Angeles Times*, January 18, 2011. http:/articles.latimes.com/2011/jan/18/entertainment/la-et-tv-pioneers-20110118.

Nichols, Nichelle. *Beyond Uhura: Star Trek and Other Memories*. New York: G. P. Putnam's Sons, 1994.

Chapter 24—Jane Juska

"A Round-Heeled Woman by Jane Juska." *The Guardian*, November 17, 2003. https:/www.theguardian.com/theguardian/2003/nov/17/digestedread.theeditorpressreview7.

Crace, John. "*Unaccompanied Women* by Jane Juska." *The Guardian*, June 19, 2006. https:/www.theguardian.com/books/2006/jun/19/digestedread.tvandradio.

Hagestadt, Emma. "Unaccompanied Women, by Jane Juska." *The Independent*, June 15, 2006. https:/www.independent.co.uk/arts-entertainment/books/reviews/unaccompanied-women-by-jane-juska-6098053.html.

Langer, Emily. "Jane Juska, Memoirist of Later-Life Sexual Pleasures, Dies at 84." *The Washington Post*, October 30, 2017. https:/www.washingtonpost.com/local/obituaries/jane-juska-memoirist-of-later-life-sexual-pleasures-dies-at-84/2017/10/30/44cf3ce0-bd7d-11e7-959c-fe2b598d8c00_story.html.

"Jane Juska: Late Literary Bloomer Who Broke Taboo of Sex and the Older Woman." *The Independent*, October 31, 2017. https:/www.independent.co.uk/news/obituaries/jane-juska-memoirist-of-sex-in-later-life-a8029041.html.

Sandomir, Richard. "Jane Juska, 84, Who Drew Notice Writing of Late-Life Sex, Dies." *The New York Times*, November 1, 2017. https:/www.nytimes.com/2017/11/01/obituaries/jane-juska-who-wrote-of-late-life-sex-dies-at-84.html.

Truss, Lynne. "Review: Memoir: A Round-Heeled Woman by Jane Juska." *The Sunday Times*, November 16, 2003. https:/www.thetimes.co.uk/article/review-memoir-a-round-heeled-woman-by-jane-juska-6q0zg5ls657.

Wilson, Frances. "The Plight of an Ageing Sensualist." *The Telegraph*, June 3, 2006. https:/www.telegraph.co.uk/culture/books/3652867/The-plight-of-an-ageing-sensualist.html.

Chapter 25—Ruth Bader Ginsburg

Farago, Jason. "Ruth Bader Ginsburg: The Supreme Court's Leading Lady Shouldn't Leave Yet." *The Guardian*, August 2, 2013. https:/www.theguardian.com/commentisfree/2013/aug/02/ruth-bader-ginsburg-supreme-court-20-years.

Ginsburg, Ruth Bader. "Ruth Bader Ginsburg's Advice for Living." *The New York Times*, October 1, 2016. https:/www.nytimes.com/2016/10/02/opinion/sunday/ruth-bader-ginsburgs-advice-for-living.html.

Senior, Jennifer. "Review: 'Notorious RBG: The Life and Times of Ruth Bader Ginsburg.'" *The New York Times*, October 23, 2015. https:/www.nytimes.com/2015/10/26/books/review-notorious-rbg-the-life-and-times-of-ruth-bader-ginsburg.html.

Toobin, Jeffrey. "Heavyweight: How Ruth Bader Ginsburg Has Moved the Supreme Court." *The New Yorker,* March 11, 2013. https:/www.newyorker.com/magazine/2013/03/11/heavyweight-ruth-bader-ginsburg.

Chapter 26—Madeleine Albright

Brockes, Emma. "I Loved What I Did." *The Guardian,* October 29, 2003. https:/www.theguardian.com/world/2003/oct/30/usa.emmabrockes.

Davies, Caroline. "Joe Just Said: 'This Marriage is Dead and I am in Love with Someone Younger and Beautiful'." *The Telegraph,* September 17, 2003. https:/www.telegraph.co.uk/news/worldnews/northamerica/usa/1441700/Joe-just-said-This-marriage-is-dead-and-I-am-in-love-with-someone-younger-and-beautiful.html.

Dobbs, Michael. "Becoming Madeleine Albright." *The Washington Post,* May 2, 1999. https:/www.washingtonpost.com/archive/lifestyle/magazine/1999/05/02/becoming-madeleine-albright/00193605-9959-442a-9f80-a6a8fd55a8bf/.

Krum, Sharon. "'I would have given up my career to save my marriage'." *The Guardian.* September 18, 2003. https:/www.theguardian.com/world/2003/sep/18/gender.uk.

Sciolino, Elaine. "Prepare for China Meeting. Buy Nonfat Yogurt." *The New York Times,* October 12, 2003. https:/www.nytimes.com/2003/10/12/books/prepare-for-china-meeting-buy-nonfat-yogurt.html.

Shelden, Michael. "Divorce Drove Me to the White House." *The Telegraph,* October 15, 2003. https:/www.telegraph.co.uk/culture/books/3604635/Divorce-drove-me-to-the-White-House.html.

Bosworth, Patricia. "Rebel without a Bra: Jane Fonda Said Her Biggest Regret Was Not Sleeping with Che Guevara.. but That Was to Please Her Husband." *The Daily Mail*, September 5, 2011. http:/www.dailymail.co.uk/femail/article-2033795/Jane-Fonda-said-biggest-regret-sleeping-Che-Guevara.html.

Fonda, Jane. *My Life So Far*. New York: Random House, 2006.

Grigoriadis, Vanessa. "Jane Fonda, Constantly Evolving." *The New York Times*, September 9, 2011. https:/www.nytimes.com/2011/09/11/books/review/jane-fonda-the-private-life-of-a-public-woman-by-patricia-bosworth-book-review.html.

Heawood, Sophie. "Jane Fonda: 'I'm 80! I keep pinching myself. I can't believe it!'" *The Guardian*, May 27, 2018. https:/www.theguardian.com/global/2018/may/27/jane-fonda-interview-film-book-club-im-80-i-cant-believe-it-racism-cosmetic-surgery.

Walter, Natasha. "The Fonda Syndrome." *The Guardian*, May 27, 2005. https:/www.theguardian.com/books/2005/may/28/featuresreviews.guardianreview1.

Chapter 28—Judge Judy Sheindlin

Barnes, Brooks. "Others Fade, but Judge Judy is Forever: At 71, She Still Presides." *The New York Times*, May 23, 1014. https:/www.nytimes.com/2014/05/24/business/media/others-fade-but-judge-judy-is-forever-at-71-she-still-presides.html.

Wetzler, Cynthia Magriel. "To Judge Judy, Standing Tall Equals Respect." *The New York Times*, April 11, 1999. http:/www.nytimes.com/1999/04/11/nyregion/to-judge-judy-standing-tall-equals-respect.html.

Marlene Wagman-Geller

Marlene Wagman-Geller received her Bachelor of Arts Degree from York University and her teaching credentials from the University of Toronto and San Diego State University. Currently, she teaches high school English in National City, California, and shares her San Diego home with her husband, Joel, daughter, Jordanna, and cat, Moe. Reviews from her first three books (Penguin/Perigree) have appeared in *The New York Times* and dozens of newspapers such as *The Denver Post*, *The Huffington Post*, and *The Chicago Tribune* which picked up an *Associated Press* article.